arctic
autumn

Houghton Mifflin Harcourt • *Boston* • *New York* • 2011

arctic
autumn

A Journey to Season's Edge

PETE DUNNE

Photos by Linda Dunne

For information about permission to reproduce selections from this book,
write to Permissions, Houghton Mifflin Harcourt Publishing Company,
215 Park Avenue South, New York, New York 10003.

www.hmhbooks.com

Library of Congress Cataloging-in-Publication Data
Dunne, Pete, date.
Arctic autumn : a journey to season's edge / Pete Dunne.
p. cm.
ISBN 978-0-618-82221-8 (hardback)
1. Natural history—Arctic regions. 2. Autumn—Arctic regions. I. Title.
QH84.1.D86 2011
508.311'3—dc23   2011016051
ISBN 978-0-618-82221-8

Book design by Anne Chalmers

Printed in the United States of America

DOC 10 9 8 7 6 5 4 3 2 1

To
BOB DITTRICK
and
LISA MOOREHEAD,
for friendship

Contents

Acknowledgments

Traveling in the Arctic takes a measure of planning and doing. Were it not for the assistance of many generous and knowledgeable folks, not only would this book never have been written but it would never have been attempted.

In particular Linda's and my gratitude is extended to Nancy and Jim DeWitt, Ted Swem, Bob and Ann Ellis, and Heimo and Edna Korth, who provided food and lodging during (or between) our travels, and John Coons, and Field Guides, Inc., for accommodating our book interests during their Pond Inlet tour of 2007.

Much of the information relating to the human and natural history of the Arctic was gleaned from other sources. There are a number of very fine books written about the Arctic, but two in particular proved most valuable and inspirational. With pleasure and due recognition, I commend them to you.

The first is *A Naturalist's Guide to the Arctic* by E. C. Pielou, essentially a backcountry bible summarizing all the extraordinary natural facets of the Arctic. The other is *The Arctic Sky: Inuit Astronomy, Star Lore, and Legend* by John MacDonald. This book is as fascinating as the culture it explores, and the information housed in its pages runs like a thread through this book.

I would also like to acknowledge the contribution that the online information resource, Wikipedia, made to this effort. While specific sources are referenced in the bibliography, I am compelled to express praise and gratitude for this colossal endeavor—a compilation of the world's knowledge placed, very literally, at the fingertips of the planet's inhabitants. Bravo!

Our travels were protracted, often requiring us to be away for weeks on end. This made extra work for my colleagues at New Jersey Audubon's Cape May Bird Observatory. My appreciation, while unbounded, still falls short of their indulgence, and my gratitude to my boss, Tom Gilmore, for granting the time away from my desk, goes beyond expression.

No book that I have written in the past quarter century has been published without an earned expression of thanks to my agent, Russell Galen (and this book is no exception). And once again I am delighted to acknowledge, and thank, my editors, Lisa White and Beth Burleigh Fuller of Houghton Mifflin Harcourt and their colleagues for making all the stages of this writing project, too, such a pleasure.

Note to Readers

Most of the experiences recounted in this book occurred as a result of travels conducted between June and November 2007—but not all. The raft trip on the Kongakut River recounted in Chapter 2 and the hunting trip in the Arctic National Wildlife Refuge, Chapter 7, occurred, respectively, in June 2006 and September–October 2008 and have been included as they would have occurred following a calendar timeline.

The Arctic is a vast and logistically challenging place. Not everything we hoped to experience and include in these pages could be tucked into a single calendar year. Anyone who has traveled in the Arctic understands this. Those who still have this adventure ahead of them will understand in time.

arctic
autumn

Chapter 1

Moon Month of Nurrait (June), "Caribou Calves"

Where Seasons Meet

Bylot Island, Nunavut, Canada

Expressions of caution and fortune exchanged, John turned
and led the rest of the members of our group back to the camp
at the mouth of the creek. As arranged, Linda and I struck out
on our own, heading west.

"How about over there?" I suggested, indicating the location of "over there" with a wave of my hand.

Linda looked in the direction I was gesturing, taking in the
snow-covered landscape, whose physical limits were defined
by a distant ridge and the sky.

"What distinguishes 'over there' from 'right here'?" she
wanted to know. Coming from the member of our team bur-

dened by thirty pounds of camera gear, it was a legitimate question and maybe one that defied a satisfactory answer. The fact was, in these early stages of the summer thaw, one part of Canada's Bylot Island looks pretty much like any other—at least any part within hiking distance.

Rising to the east were mountains whose color and pattern made them look like they'd been cast from scoops of vanilla fudge ice cream—but cheap vanilla fudge. The kind where they skimp on the fudge.

To the north, bracketed by peaks, was the Aktineaq Glacier, one of the many ice sheets for which Canada's 22,252-square-kilometer Sirmilik National Park is named. Sirmilik, in the Inuktitut language of the native Inuit people, means "Place of Glaciers."

To the west, somewhere beyond the visual limits of "over there," was a marshy plain that serves as the nesting ground for the world's largest breeding colony of greater snow geese.

To the south, across twenty-five frozen miles of Eclipse Sound, was Baffin Island, the largest island in the Canadian Arctic Archipelago and home to the majority of the mostly Native residents of Canada's newest, and northernmost, province, Nunavut.

There are very few places on the planet where you can look south onto Baffin Island, and, among the planet's nearly 7 billion human inhabitants, only a fraction might ever have dreamed of doing so.

One of them was me. One of them was Linda. But wasn't the other one you?

Yes, you. The onetime bright and slightly bored kid slouched in one of those plastic desk chairs that ruined the backs of a whole generation. Didn't you used to sit in class and stare, wistfully, at the pull-down map of the world covering the blackboard and marvel at that patchwork of islands way up there at the top of the world?

A fragmented land whose color was no color at all. Not red or green or yellow like all the other landforms on the map but white!

Snow white. Arctic white.

Didn't you, as the disciplines that would turn us into well-adjusted and productive members of society were being instilled, study those northern lands and dream of being the adventurer every kid, deep in his heart, knows himself to be?

Sure you did. There's a little bit of Robert Service and Admiral Peary in all of us.

And haven't you, during all the responsible and productive adult years that followed, feasted upon the pages of travel and nature magazines in barbershops and hair salons (and chiropractic center waiting rooms), thrilling to images of those Arctic lands?

Polar bears cradling cubs so winsome a panda could die of envy.

Caribou herds so vast they filled whole treeless valleys and spilled into the next.

Lilliputian flowers carpeting landscapes whose limits were fixed by the sky.

And didn't you, until the receptionist called your name, rekindle those classroom ambitions and vow that someday—when the kids were raised, when the house was paid off—you would finally become the explorer you were meant to be and head. . .

"Over there," I said, in answer to Linda's question, "will give us a much better view to the west." It was a promise without foundation. Fact is, like you, I'd never been "over there" either, had no freaking idea what we might find. Linda greeted this explanation with silence.

"What we're looking for is the place where everything comes together. Spring, summer, autumn, winter. A seasonal and geographic crossroads. A high point and a tipping point, symbolic of summer's greatest advance and winter's final stronghold."

Silence.

"Like that point over there," I said, pointing, once again, toward a volcano-shaped mound mantling a distant ridge.

"That is *not* an *over there*," Linda pronounced. "That is an *up there*. And to get *up* there, we have to first slog across that low, wet marshy area *down there*. Even from here I can hear the gurgle of water flowing under what has to be some pretty rotten spring ice."

Impressed and amused, I studied the pack-burdened form that was my wife—five feet, two inches of blond-haired, hazel-eyed, set-jawed indomitableness. We've been married over twenty years, traveling much of the time. She can walk, kayak, and photograph all day and then, in the evening, edit the day's crop of images. She's as organized as I am not and as patient as I am exasperating. In addition to being a wonderful partner, she is an accomplished outdoor traveler whose background includes stints as a park ranger in Alaska, an instructor for the National Outdoor Leadership School in Wyoming, and over a dozen wilderness trips in the Arctic.

In short, she's the kind of person whose counsel (and objections) is worth listening to, whether you are traveling in the Arctic or not.

"You're not part Inuit, are you?" I accused.

"No," she said, letting some of her exasperation show with a slouch.

"You really think it's too wet down there?" I said.

"No," she corrected. "I just said it *was* wet and I wanted to know how important it is to go 'up there' before we find out *how* wet."

"I do think the photo ops will be better up there," I offered. "Down here you're shooting in a bowl; up there we'll be on top of the world."

The photographer in Linda didn't exactly rise to the bait, but she didn't dismiss my analysis either.

"We can try it," she said, at last. "But we're going to have to hurry. It's only an hour until the solstice. Distance is hard to judge in the Arctic, and I'll bet 'up there' is farther than it looks."

We did hurry. And the terrain, for once, turned out to be not as bad as it looked. And now you know why Linda and I had flown twenty-four hundred miles from our home in New Jersey, been shaken *and stirred* for thirty miles over open ice in a snowmobile-drawn sled, and hiked five more just to be here. We were set to mark the onset of autumn, and begin the third book in our season series at the place where seasons meet.

That place, recent reconnaissance suggested, lay "up there."

AUTUMN?

I know what you are thinking. Anybody who studied maps and dreamed of being an explorer certainly knows that June 21, the date of the solstice, usually marks the first day of summer, not autumn—and so it does! Technically and in fact.

At 1806 Greenwich Mean Time, or 2:06 Eastern daylight-saving time—the politically adjusted time zone in which Bylot Island lies—the earth's annual journey around the sun would reach one of its quarterly milestones: the point at which the Northern Hemisphere inclines at its maximum angle toward the sun.

On this date, all points on and north of the Arctic Circle (66 degrees, 33 minutes north latitude) enjoy twenty-four hours of full sunlight. Were you to watch all day, you'd see the sun go completely around the sky and never dip below the horizon.

At 71 degrees, 5 minutes north latitude, the coordinates of southern Bylot Island, we would be so entertained.

Also on this date, at noon, at all points above the tropic of Cancer (23.5 degrees north latitude), the sun reaches its highest point in the sky. Inhabitants experience the longest day of the year. The Northern Hemisphere receives a maximum amount of solar insolation.

It is the pinnacle of summer! Tipping point, too. Because also technically and in fact, it's all downhill from here. The day following the solstice finds the sun lower in the sky. All points lying directly on the Arctic Circle will see the sun dip below the horizon, and each successive day will see this period of disappearance increase.

Day by day, less sunlight reaches the Northern Hemisphere. Day by day, the Arctic retreats deeper and faster into winter. The midpoint on this seasonal descent marks another quarterly milestone. It occurs on September 22 or 23. It is called the autumnal equinox. Across the most heavily populated portions of the Northern Hemisphere, very probably where you live, relatively mild temperatures prevail.

Not so at the earth's Arctic region. Because on that first official day of autumn, the sun does not appear at the North Pole at all. On the Arctic Circle, where the day is evenly divided between twelve hours of daylight and twelve hours of darkness, at noon the sun rises a mere 23.5 degrees above the southern horizon, shedding light but little warmth on the earth below.

In Fort Yukon, an Alaskan village lying just north of the Arctic Circle, the average daily high temperature in late September is in the low forties, and at night, the thermometer dips to the upper teens or low twenties. At Pond Inlet, the native village visible just across the channel, the average daily temperature in late September is in the low twenties.

Summer in the Arctic is transforming but ephemeral. Autumn comes early and surrenders quickly. All of the Arctic's denizens, both the hardy ones that migrate seasonally and the hardier ones that remain year-round, accelerate their schedules accordingly.

"All birds gone in September" is how one of our Inuit guides expressed it.

Gone where? South. Fleeing to temperate lands where the sun is a year-round resident, not a timid visitor.

So here on Bylot Island, high above the Arctic Circle, June 21 not only celebrates the first day of summer but also marks the first day of fall. The day the sun begins its retreat, and the earth begins its six-month slide into the Inuit moon month of Tauvikjuaq, "the Great Darkness."

POINT OF DEPARTURE

We struck out for the ridge, walking for the most part across soft, granular snow—ankle-deep in some places, knee-deep in others. And while there certainly were places where we would have been, as Linda put it, "up to our crotches in ice water," with caution and fortune we avoided them.

"How are you doing back there?" I hailed over my left shoulder when the crunch of Linda's footsteps faltered.

"Fine," she said over my right shoulder.

I turned to find her kneeling in slush, camera in hand, macro lens flirting with a spray of tundra flowers poking through the snow. During the next few weeks, as winter snow surrenders to the power of twenty-four-hour sunlight, the tundra would become one great floral display: a flower show unrivaled on Earth.

Heather and mosses dominate in lower, wetter areas; lichen in the higher, drier, rockier places. Tight clusters of furry-stemmed woolly lousewort and purple-colored saxifrage, like the one beneath Linda's lens, were just beginning to impart touches of color to the winter landscape.

But one plant conspicuously absent on Bylot Island is trees. In fact, the absence of woody plants is one of the defining characteristics of the Arctic environment and the tundra biome that dominates it. The very name *tundra* comes from the Finnish word *tunturi*, which means "treeless plain."

The Arctic, whose name's root is the Greek word *arktikos*, meaning "near the bear" (the constellation Ursa Minor, which includes Polaris, the North Star), is a tough proving ground for living things. To qualify as tundra plants, flora must be able to endure long months without sunlight, prolonged cold that would freeze the ambitions of lesser plants, and winds that whip and desiccate.

Finding water, too, is a problem, because annual rainfall is scant across much of the Arctic (a desertlike six to ten inches a year), and for much of that year, water is in a form that plants find hard to assimilate: ice. Even at the height of summer, ice, or permafrost, lies mere inches below the earth's surface. Root structures that serve to anchor tall plants find no footing, so trees have no standing.

In order to meet the challenges of the Arctic environment, plants tend to be small, ground-hugging, often "furry," fast-growing, and commonly rooted in sheltering clusters. Many are dark, to absorb sunlight. Some retain their leaves through winter to start the process of photosynthesis as soon as sunlight finds them. Many flowers produce buds in the fall so they are ready to bloom at the first touch of spring. With a growing season limited to fifty to sixty days, every advantage is an advantage.

While the tundra plant community thrives where it is too cold and the growing season too short for grasslands or forest, it is not entirely correct to call it "*tunturi*." In sheltered places, there are ground-hugging willows—trees that have abandoned their woody plant pride to embrace the earth like vines. The competitive advantage enjoyed by trees—the pectin-stiffened stalks that allow them to climb above lesser plants and hog all the sunlight—doesn't serve them in the Arctic. There's plenty of sunlight during the brief Arctic growing season—at least enough for plants to grow leaves, roots, and the flowers and seeds that are their vehicles for procreation. There just isn't enough time and sunlight to produce wood, too.

So, except for dwarf willows, trees are essentially nonexistent in this biome. In fact, and from an ecological standpoint, the absence of trees is commonly used to mark the boundaries of the Arctic environment—a demarcation called the "tree line." It traces and defines the northern limit of the vast boreal forest, the earth's last great forest biome. On that pulldown classroom map, this ecological boundary appears as a dotted line wandering across northern Canada, Norway, Sweden, Finland, Russia, and Alaska. In some places, the tree line extends north of the Arctic Circle, the geographic boundary of the Arctic. For example, in the Canadian Yukon, the tree line extends almost to the Beaufort Sea. In other places, the tree line plunges south of the circle. Churchill, Manitoba, located at 58 degrees, 46 minutes, 9 seconds north latitude and known as the "Polar Bear Capital of the World," lies right at tree line.

Over oceans, the Arctic boundary line traces the fifty Fahrenheit isotherm, a line that falls along the point where the average July high temperature is below fifty degrees Fahrenheit. This boundary encompasses the extreme North Atlantic and most of the Bering Sea. It also means that southern Greenland, Iceland, and islands like St. Lawrence and the Pribilofs lie within the Arctic region.

Bylot Island, at 73 degrees, 16 minutes north latitude, lies well above the tree line. In fact, it falls in a habitat zone that is known as the "High Arctic"—where all the seasons meet and where, for a few short weeks, all vie and none dominate.

Like Linda said, it's a picture that says it all. Last year's cotton grass. This year's saxifrage. A landscape still mostly covered by winter's snow. A waxing sun approaching the peak of its hemispheric climb.

All the elements were here. Old and new, beginnings and endings all present and accounted for. All we needed, now, was a point of departure and a tipping point in time.

· · ·

PINGO!

We reached the volcano-shaped hummock, or pingo, with ten minutes to spare, and the view, as hoped, was worth the climb. We weren't the first to appreciate it.

"Snowy owl pellets," Linda noted, pointing toward the large weathered rock that served as the hilltop's highest point.

"Look old," I noted, going over to the lichen-encrusted stone. Picking up several of the fur and bone castings. Subjecting them to the probing of an opposable thumb and a human intellect—the two game-changing advantages our species brings to bear.

"*Lemmus defunctus,*" I pronounced, with more sagacity than I was entitled to. I'm no small mammal expert. But playing the odds, reconstituted lemming, the small rodent that makes up the predatory prey base of the Arctic, was almost certainly the principal ingredient of the regurgitated capsule. The question was, which species of lemming?

Collared lemming, which turns white in winter and prefers drier areas, or brown lemming, which remains dark-furred all year and favors wetter tundra. Brown lemming is also the species that goes through the cyclic population peaks and crashes that have made the name lemming a metaphor for mass hysteria and self-destruction.

The myth-busting truth is, lemmings do not engage in mass suicide, running pell-mell over cliffs. What they do is outstrip their resources, bringing upon themselves a population collapse that draws predator populations down with them. In the Arctic, as elsewhere, all living things are intertwined. What affects one affects others.

Collared lemming populations also fluctuate but less dramatically. Able to strike a balance with their environment that is more sustaining and sustainable, they avoid the boom-and-bust cycles of their relatives.

Our species could learn a great deal from collared lemmings, big brains or no. But when it comes to population dynamics, evidence suggests we have more in common with the other rodent.

"Hey, in all that Harry Potter mania, did anyone ever mention the fact that snowy owls puke up their dinner?"

"Not that I recall," Linda, who was alternately checking her camera settings and her watch, replied. "What lens do you think I should use?"

"To take a picture of owl pellets?"

"To take a picture of you worshiping the sun. Isn't that why we came up here? By the way, it's 2:01. We've got five minutes. Four and a half for you to decide whether to sit or stand."

I chose to sit. On the lichen-stained rock. If it was good enough for a snowy owl, it was certainly good enough for a snowy owl admirer.

"Are you going to just sit there?" Linda asked.

"I guess. What do you want me to do?"

"Look around. Scan. Search for wildlife or for the Northwest Passage or something. It's been every Arctic explorer's dream for five hundred years."

So I did. Brought binoculars to my eyes. Scoured the Arctic for signs of life. Found little, relatively speaking. There were several reasons for this.

First, Bylot Island was experiencing a late spring. Many of the waterfowl and shorebirds that breed here had yet to arrive. Snow still dominated the landscape, and snow-covered tundra doesn't accommodate most nesting birds.

My search disclosed a single pair of newly arrived American golden-plovers just south of our (and probably their) pingo, eyeing us skeptically. To the north, a single pair of white-rumped sandpipers were making the air buzz with their courtship gyrations.

Even though Bylot Island constitutes a breeding stronghold for these and other long-distance migrants, breeding density in the Arctic is low. The Arctic is indeed a great bird hatchery, but it is also an immense bird hatchery. When white-rumps and other shorebirds arrive, they spread out. People who are used to seeing massed flocks of shorebirds during migration will not find them here.

Also, it was not a good lemming year. You didn't need to conduct a population study to ascertain this. The absence of snowy owls, Arctic foxes, and the relatively few jaegers about said it all. Predators go where they find prey, and this year they weren't finding it on Bylot Island.

There was one last but very determining reason why Linda and I were not overwhelmed by hosts of living things. This is that we were standing at the evolutionary end of the line. Not only do the seasons founder at 73 degrees 16 minutes north, but so, too, does the kingdom of living things.

Relatively few plants, insects, birds, and mammals have managed to push the limits of adaptation to accommodate the rigors of the High Arctic. In North America there are approximately seven hundred species of breeding birds. On Bylot Island, there are thirty-five. Only one bird species in twenty was tough enough to make the evolutionary cut.

If you want a more poignant example, consider the relative abundance of reptiles and amphibians on Bylot Island.

Across North America, there are approximately six hundred herps. On Bylot Island, and throughout the Arctic, there are precisely none.

So you might fairly ask why two avid naturalists would choose to anchor a book that purports to engage natural wonders in such a biologically impoverished place.

"Two-minute warning," Linda announced. "There's a rough-legged hawk doing a courtship display over that cliff behind you," she added.

Okay, that's one reason. The reason we, and the many celebrated naturalists and explorers who preceded us, traveled to the Arctic end of the earth is that there are marvels to be found here that cannot be found anywhere else.

If you want to see a narwhal, the whale whose lancelike tusk inspired the unicorn myth, you have no alternative but to travel to the icy waters of the Arctic.

We did. Saw fifty animals diving and surfacing in the slushy edge of the winter ice floe. It was incredible. For both of us, one of those encounters you dream of, then live for, then use as a measure of accomplishment to mark the passage of your life.

If you want to see a polar bear, the planet's largest land carnivore, you have no choice but to go to the edge of the Arctic ice, where the "ice bear" makes its living.

We did. Watched a female and her half-grown cub pick up our scent, change course, and close to within a quarter mile of our group. Close enough so that through a spotting scope we could peer down the dark chasm behind her open, swinging jaws. Close enough to hear the bawled protest of her cub as she led him to the edge of the ice sheet and across the open channel to the pack ice beyond.

And if you want to see rough-legged hawks courting. If you

want to see red-throated loons in their maroon-throated finery. If you want to see caribou calves braving their first river crossing. Peer into the fathomless eyes of a female gyrfalcon on her nest ledge. Smack Arctic foxes on the nose with your hat to keep them from pilfering your lunch. Or if you want to stand on a frost-scoured hilltop, with the sound of utter silence pressing into your ears, and survey an area the size of a Texas county that has not been compromised by a communications tower, an oil derrick, a jet contrail, there are very few places on this earth you can still go.

But one of them is that place you used to stare at. On that pull-down map. When your dreams were more abundant than your memories and perhaps now, at this late stage of your life, more alluring, too.

"One minute," Linda announced.

Which brings up a related matter. Life is both cheap and precious precisely and ironically for the same reason. It is finite. You are likely old enough to have suffered losses of your own: family, friends. Maybe you have survived serious illness or are nursing a "condition." If so, you know how cheaply death trades and how unpredictable life is.

The American writer John Steinbeck, who never saw the Arctic but who was, nonetheless, an attentive student of both people and nature, once observed that if you want to make a flower appear really blue, gild it with an edge of white. This wisdom applies to life, and it might be that this was Steinbeck's metaphoric intent, because if you want to make life seem really precious, set it against the unforgiving starkness of the Arctic.

A snow bunting, perched defiantly atop a stone spire ten thousand wind-stropped years in the making, will break your heart. A sow grizzly, flanked by cubs, navigating a path between sun-lacquered hilltops and a rain-cloud-darkened sky, will make you believe that your faith in the enduring richness of this planet was never misplaced.

"Ready?" Linda said.

If all these reasons are not enough to make you break with the routine of your life and set off to explore the world beyond your own, here is one more. Because there once was a child who looked a bit like you. They sat in front of a map in a classroom that lies an adult's lifetime away. And inside this child was the soul of an explorer who never got the chance to explore. Unless you act, it never will.

For the record, the solstice occurred right on schedule, at 2:06 P.M. EDST. Nothing happened except that the Northern Hemisphere, which for 182 ½ days had been inching toward summer, reversed course and started heading the other way. And two explorers, poised atop an unnamed ridge in the Canadian Arctic, started their journey into autumn together.

Meanwhile, twenty-four hundred miles to the south, in Cumberland County, New Jersey, which Linda and I call home, the first southbound short-billed dowitchers were setting their wings and dropping into the marshes of Delaware Bay. For these Arctic nesters, whose breeding range lies east of Hudson Bay and south of Bylot Island, the short breeding season was already over. Like the earth in her orbit, like Linda and me, the first of the Arctic's denizens were beginning their journey into autumn, too.

THE TASTE OF LONG-TAILEDS

By morning, our last day on the ice, the gulf of water lying between the floe edge and the pack ice had widened considerably. But the yodeling clamor of long-tailed ducks was un-diminished. It was the sound that greeted our group of birders when our snowmobile-drawn sleds had reached the rotting edge of the ice, two days before. It was the last sound we heard as we zipped up our sleeping bags and surrendered to sleep. The first sound we heard when we woke. And very probably the audible pulse of it throbbed in our dreams as we slept through the darkless night of late June.

To the Inuit, the arrival of these rakish sea ducks is synonymous with spring. Their departure heralds the imminence of winter. If you wanted to pick the poster bird for the Arctic breeding season, the long-tailed duck would certainly be a contender. If you concluded that this plume-tailed bird is a favorite of mine, you would not be mistaken.

Coffee mug in hand, directing my steps as much as possible into the sound-dampening puddles of meltwater, I made my way from the cook tent to the observation point fifty feet short of the floe edge. Behind me was our tent encampment and sleeping company. Before me the edge of the Arctic ice sheet, the place where winter was holding the line and would until well into July, when the last of the seasonal icecap would melt.

I'm an early riser, have been all my life. As a kid growing up in suburban North Jersey, I was often out exploring the woods behind my parents' home at dawn. Hours later I'd be sitting on the steps of our porch, still waiting for the first of my neighborhood playmates to emerge.

Now, better than fifty years into this pattern, I've grown accustomed to having the morning to myself. So I was surprised to see Matthias sitting beside the tarp-covered sled where he had spent the night. Cigarette in an ungloved hand. Aboriginal-black eyes focused on the sea ice at his booted feet.

Weather-cured, mahogany-dark face set beneath cropped black hair touched by gray.

I don't mean to imply that the Inuit lead indolent lives. On the contrary, the productive use of time is part of the Arctic people's pattern and temperament. Half a century of Canadian government–imposed centralization has not eclipsed the habits imparted by centuries of nomadic hunting tradition. But during the weeks of twenty-four-hour sunlight that Arctic dwellers enjoy, there is a natural tendency to stay up and rise late. In summer, in government-established towns like Pond Inlet and seasonal hunting and fishing camps alike, stirring before midmorning is more the exception among Native people than the norm.

Perhaps, being oldest among our guides, Matthias didn't need as much sleep as the younger drivers. Or perhaps, being leader, and responsible for our safety, he had things on his mind.

John Coons, who was handling the bird-watching end of our five-day tour, recalled to us the time Matthias abruptly uprooted their camp at the edge of the ice and relocated the group a mile closer to land. The wind was shifting. He didn't like it.

Next morning, the group awoke to find that, during the night, the landscape they'd evacuated had gone from ice to open sea. With so much riding on the wisdom and experience of Matthias, I limited my intrusion upon his privacy to a raised mug and a nod of greeting, which he returned.

Back in Pond Inlet, while Matthias was organizing the loading of passengers and gear, I'd asked his nephew, another driver, how old his uncle was.

"Forty-five to sixty-five," he'd confided after a moment's reflection and no indication that the lack of specificity was the least bit odd. But accepting the high-end estimate meant that Matthias, like many elders in the village of Pond Inlet, would have been born before the Canadian government relocated the aboriginal people into towns.

What this means, then, is that Matthias would most likely have been born in an igloo, if his birth date fell in late autumn or winter, or in a skin tent if he was born in the spring or summer—a period heralded by the arrival of the *aggiarjuit* (AKA *aggiajuk*), the long-tailed duck. In fact, in the gaming spirit of the Inuit people, those who are born in tents are known as *aggiarjuits*. Those who are born in igloos fall under the banner of the *aqiggiit*, the ptarmigan, a hardy species that lives in the Arctic all year—one of the very few bird species to do so.

The *aggiarjuits* and the *aqiggiits*. The tent fraternity versus the igloo folks. It's a little like going to summer camp and being divided into the red team and the blue team, except in Inuit society, the labels last for life.

I guessed Matthias was an *aqiggiit*. He didn't look much like a long-tailed duck.

Where do real long-tailed ducks spend the balance of their lives when the short Arctic breeding season is over and winter reclaims the North? They retreat to the shallow, coastal waters of the Atlantic and Pacific, including the coast of New Jersey, where Linda and I live. Among Delaware baymen, the bird has a different name. There it is known as the . . .

South southerly, south southerly, south southerly . . .

The nasal mantra of love-struck long-tailed ducks grew louder as I approached the floe edge. There were hundreds of birds pressed close to the ice. Many more swimming beyond. Flagellum-tailed males and chunky females. One bird driven to song would ignite a chorus. The resulting clamor drowned out the crooning moan of eiders and the wail of red-throated loons, whose numbers were likewise impressive—in the hundreds, maybe thousands.

In fact the open water was fairly churning with ducks and seabirds, each and every one impatient for the sun to thaw the tundra ponds where the birds, most already paired, would breed. The birds had migrated hundreds, some thousands, of miles, overflying the advancing edge of spring itself. Here, they waited for the season to catch up, but they didn't wait quietly.

By the way, you don't have to travel all the way to the Arctic to hear long-tailed ducks. The birds begin their pair bonding in January and February. If you are unfamiliar with the call, then you have been cheated of one of the greatest sounds in nature. Its cadence is akin to the beating of a human heart. You may not know the sound, but the rhythm is in your blood. The tone has a nasal vibrancy that seems to hum in the soul, an Arctic *om*. It sounds, at once, both urgent and comical. It fills you with life and it makes you laugh.

As the Inuit laugh. In fact, almost a third of the conversation among our drivers seemed taken up by laughter.

But "south southerly"?

In a place that lies at 73 degrees, 16 minutes north latitude, the name is more than a little incongruous. The eastern end of Bylot Island lies north of almost everything and south of very little. The closest human enclave, our expedition's point of departure, was the hamlet of Pond Inlet—a community of fourteen hundred souls located at the northern tip of Baffin Island. It ranks among the northernmost communities on Earth.

But long-tailed ducks breed even farther north than this, at the northern tip of Ellesmere Island, about as far as land goes before it founders in ice. Like those of many Arctic species, the duck's breeding range is circumpolar—occupying all the northern lands ringing the pole, ignoring the distinction of continents and political boundaries.

But while long-tailed ducks swear no allegiance to flags, they live as all Arctic creatures do, at the sufferance of winter. Spring, as noted, was running late—seven to ten days by the estimates of our guides. The freshwater tundra ponds that long-tailed ducks nest beside remained locked in ice.

In the High Arctic, winter rules, or, as our drivers expressed it, "Ice is the boss." A quick spring melts into a brief summer; summer hardens into an early fall. Some years, summer doesn't really happen at all. Birds come north, meet only ice and snow, turn around and start back.

On the Edge

I stopped just shy of the crack marking the point where the next section of winter ice was getting ready to sever ties and join the floating pack ice about half a mile out. The crack had widened overnight—wide enough to permit thick-billed murres, traveling beneath the six-foot-thick ice, to forage. Wide enough so that even the dumbest among our tour group could see the danger it presented.

Two days earlier this had not been the case. In fact, members of our group had wandered to within two feet of the snow-covered opening before one of the drivers sauntered over, exposing the hidden danger with a probe.

This morning, there was just a thin crust of snow over the crevasse. It was this crust that betrayed Matthias's approach. Tearing my eyes from the spectacle of birds, I looked over my shoulder to find him walking my way. A short, powerfully built man wearing a faded blue barn coat and sun-bleached reddish rain pants. His gait, part amble, part limp, suggested that some of his wisdom had been hard-bought.

He acknowledged my presence by stopping when he reached my shoulder. He wasn't unfriendly, merely focused, and his focus had to do with perceiving the elements of the world around him. I've spent a lot of time with people who make their living out-of-doors, but I have never met a people so empathetically attuned to their environment as the Inuit. You don't live on the ice and reach the age of Matthias without being able to perceive, assess, and react to the world around you. You don't get to be an elder, or a leader, without cause.

At the time of our expedition, the people of Pond Inlet were coming to terms with the loss of one of their elders— an eighty-one-year-old hunter who a week earlier had gone off, alone, to hunt seal and never returned. The gas can he'd cached to fuel his trip back was found on the ice. But the man and his snow machine were not.

No, Matthias wasn't being unfriendly. In fact, just the opposite. He was donning the mantle of Arctic ambassador. Engaging a person whose environmental reflexes were conditioned in the more hospitable south and whose cultural heritage lay to Europe, the east. The Inuit migrated across Arctic Alaska and Canada from the west. The first time East met

West was one thousand years ago and not far south of where Matthias and I stood now.

One thousand years ago, as now, the earth was enjoying a period of global warming—a brief respite in what has been a protracted period of cooler temperatures and periodic glaciation going back perhaps 2.5 million years. Changing climates result in geographic shifts in the planet's biota, and two of those shifts involved two different peoples, two different cultures. One, the Inuit (or Inupiat, as they are called in Alaska), who moved east, out of Alaska, displacing an older, Dorset people, who were already established in what would one day become Arctic Canada. The other colonizing people were the Norse (more romantically called the "Vikings"), who migrated west, out of Scandinavia, settling in Iceland, Greenland, and, for a brief time, the New World. A place they named "Vineland."

In 986, a Norse adventurer named Bjarni Herjolfsson set off from Iceland to join a contingent of Norse colonists, led by Erik the Red, who had emigrated to the southern end of a large and attractively named landmass to the west called "Greenland." Bjarni overshot not only the colony but the landmass and found himself and his ship skirting the edge of land that seemed not to fit the description of its name. The land he discovered had trees. Greenland, like Bylot Island, does not. Sailing first north, where the land became increasingly treeless, the wanderers then turned east, finding eventually Greenland and the Norse colony.

Fourteen years later, in the same boat and intrigued by Herjolfsson's story of a land to the west, Erik the Red's son, Leif Eriksson, sailed west, landing first in Helluland (Baffin

Island) before turning south, retracing Bjarni's route, reaching and spending the winter in what is now northeastern Newfoundland.

The very first meeting of the New World Inuit (called "*skraelingar*" or "*scraelings*" by the Norse) and the prospecting Norse is unrecorded, but contact is a certainty, and trade was one of the byproducts. A short-lived settlement (in L'Anse aux Meadows, Newfoundland) and three centuries of trade for the ivory the Norse coveted and the iron the Inuit wanted attest to it. The end of this period of economic exchange, the first to link the human community across the planet, came with the onset of the Little Ice Age, a period of global cooling that began in the 1400s and resulted in the abandonment of the Norse Greenland colonies—the "Old World's" jump-off point to the New.

But contact between the Inuit and western society was, from this point, more or less ongoing. Basque fishermen, lured north by the region's cod-rich waters, were fishing off Labrador by the sixteenth century. In 1576, the English sea captain Martin Frobisher's search for the Northwest Passage resulted in the first documented meeting of northern Native and European people when his ship landed on Baffin Island. Nevertheless, the harshness and remoteness of the Arctic severely limited European influence until the beginning of the twentieth century. And it really wasn't until the middle part of that century that the full weight of western culture came crashing down on the Inuit.

While the Native people could thrive in a cold climate, they were culturally undone by the Cold War—a decades-long conflict between the Soviet Union and the United States and its ally Canada—in which the Arctic became strategically important. Periodic contact with missionaries, traders, and a scattering of Royal Canadian Mounted Police gave way to unremitting cultural contact as air bases and radar outpost sites were constructed across the Canadian and Alaskan Arctic.

In the 1950s, the Canadian government initiated a policy of relocation, directing Native peoples to abandon their many seasonal encampments and concentrate, permanently, in government-built centers. The avowed purpose was to alleviate hunger among Native peoples and offer them and their children the manifest benefits of western civilization. The underlying objective was to assert Canadian dominion over the now-strategic northern regions.

The result was that a nomadic, hunting culture was subverted. By the time Linda and I arrived, only elders like Matthias could boast unbroken linkage to the traditional ways of what were, arguably, the world's greatest hunting people—a culture that was also adept in the use of nets and weirs.

"Fish," Matthias said, pointing with one hand toward the two murres feeding in the crack, extending the thumb and index finger of the other to express small size. An entire conversation boiled down to one word and two gestures.

Their apparent disregard for the human aging process notwithstanding, the Inuit are a direct and precise people—particularly when it comes to the elements of the world around them. Their language shows an elevated genius for giving directions or pinpointing locations (the map of the region on the wall of the Pond Inlet library shows a name for virtually every geographic nuance). But such linguistic precision works against verbosity.

The full conversation might have gone like this.

"Matthias, what are those birds eating?"

"The two birds in the crack in the ice?"

"Yes, those two birds."

"They are eating small fish approximately two inches long."

But Matthias's one-word pronouncement said all this and more. It demonstrated that he'd correctly gauged my curiosity and honored me with the assumption that I was attentive enough to have noticed the murres in the first place.

Honesty compels me to admit that there were probably two other considerations accounting for Matthias's minimalist approach to conversation. First, as for most older Inuit, for Matthias English is a second language. At home, among his people, conversations are held in the Native Inuktitut tongue. Second, Matthias was hard of hearing. His right ear hosted a hearing aid—a testimony to right-handedness and a token to his many years hunting seals with a high-caliber rifle and no ear protection.

Not that these deficiencies impeded conversation. In fact, over the course of the next five minutes I learned more about birds that I am supposed to know than during any other five-minute period in my life. I was even to discover the answer to a question that has dogged me for more than a decade.

After his pronouncement concerning the murres and their prey, Matthias turned to read my face and seemed happy to note the spark of understanding.

"Smelt," I said, anyway, because I come from a verbal culture and because it is my discipline to pin names to things.

Matthias nodded. "Lays one egg," he said (of the murres, not the smelt). "Big egg," he added, with relish.

This disclosure certified not only his ornithological credentials but their practical roots. The fact is, not one bird watcher in a thousand could tell you how many eggs murres lay. Bird watching is big on finding and identifying birds but gives biological insight short shrift. In part because not disturbing birds while they are nesting is something of an ethic among birders, also because the practice of egging (i.e., harvesting the eggs of migrating birds for food) is illegal.

Unless you happen to enjoy an aboriginal background. If you looked on the map in the Pond Inlet library, you would note that about four miles above Button Point there are "bird cliffs," a colony in which murres, and other cliff-nesting seabirds, abound. Murres do indeed lay a single, large egg. The Inuit have prized murre eggs for food for centuries.

Not coincidentally, in the Inuit calendar, which is based upon the same thirteen-month lunar cycle as the ancient Romans', the twenty-eight-day lunar period bracketing late June into July is called Mannitt, in Inuktitut, "Egg." It coincides with that time when newly arrived migrating birds are laying eggs, and the best time for harvesting them.

Most of the names of the months in the Inuit calendar relate to some biological phenomenon indicative of that time frame. April–May is Nattian or "seal pup." September–October, Amiraijaut, the shedding of velvet from caribou antlers. To the Inuit, there is no distinction between their world and the natural world. The challenge is surviving in it.

"That one," Matthias said, indicating a common eider feeding near the ice, "three egg.

"That one," he said, pointing now to a female long-tailed duck, "six egg.

"Come in April," he added. Then, pointing to a northern fulmar, "That one come in April"; then thick-billed murre, "That one come in April."

"Leave in September," he said, and there was a pause. "All birds leave in September," he pronounced. As well they should. By late September, in the moon month Amiraijaut, ponds are freezing and snow is beginning to accumulate in the High Arctic. By late October and early November, sea ice begins to form.

This is the moon month of Ukiulirut, which means "winter starts."

I was writing as Matthias spoke, and, for one petty moment, I thought about checking the accuracy of his estimates of clutch size against scientific literature. I decided against it. Frankly, if there was shown to be a discrepancy, my money would be on the guy who doesn't distinguish his world from the natural world. That's when it hit me. Matthias would almost certainly have the answer to a question that had been bugging me for years.

During the nineties I wrote a biweekly column for the New Jersey Sunday section of the *New York Times*. One of those columns had to do with long-tailed ducks, then called "old squaws," a pejorative label ascribed to early French trappers, who are alleged to have heard the birds on their breeding territories and likened the clamor to the gossiping of "old squaws."

As mentioned, long-tailed ducks are common wintering birds along the Atlantic Coast, from Virginia to Newfoundland. During the writing, I got to wondering what the birds tasted like.

Like most humans, meat figures in my diet. Unlike many people, I still adhere to one of our species' oldest interspecific practices. I hunt. And while I've never hunted sea ducks, I know people who do.

So I sought the counsel of one of my duck-hunting friends, a decoy carver named Jim Seibert (whose long-tailed duck carvings are works of art worthy of an Inuit craftsman).

"Hell, I've never eaten one of the things," Jim informed me. "But I know a carver on Long Beach Island who's eaten them. Why don't you give him a call?" Which I did, only to learn that he, too, had "never eaten one of the things." However, he did know a hunter on Long Island . . .

Who it turned out had also "never eaten one of the things" but knew somebody on Cape Cod . . .

Who knew somebody in Down East Maine . . .

Who knew somebody in Nova Scotia . . .

My epicurean quest finally ended in Newfoundland with a gentleman who, likewise, had "never eaten one of the things," and who could think of no other authority on the subject I might question.

"Matthias," I said, pointing. "How does that one taste?"

"Tastes good," he said, without hesitation. Then he added "That one tastes *very* good."

That a man of such few words would have mustered so many in his reply can only be a testimony to the epicurean elegance of the bird.

While it is fascinating that two cultures could regard the bird so differently, it is hardly surprising. To most Americans, the Arctic, and the traditions of its people, is only slightly less alien than the moon. They'll never go there. They see no reason to go there. They perceive no link between themselves and a corner of the world that is, for much of the year, locked in ice and snow.

But what these many estranged members of my culture fail to recognize is how closely tied the Arctic is to their lives. Like the long-tailed duck, many of the birds that are found across the continental United States and southern Canada in winter breed in the Arctic.

The American tree sparrow coming to a suburban Connecticut bird feeder and the snow geese hunted in coastal Texas all herald from the Arctic. Winter snow and ice reflecting sunlight back into space serve as a planetary thermoregulator, and the permafrost underlying the tundra functions as a giant carbon dioxide reservoir, bottling up a climate-changing dose of this greenhouse gas.

The Arctic might be distant, but it is hardly disjunct. And the impact from environmental changes occurring there now will most certainly strike close to home in the near and distant future no matter where on this planet your home may be.

Matthias's disclosure regarding long-tailed duck appeared to signal the end of our conversation. Administering the camp, not interpreting nature, was his principal concern. He turned without a word of, or need for, apology and ambled back to camp, where some of the early-rising members of our group were beginning to muster, swaying like a polar bear crosses ice or, perhaps, a sea duck crosses land.

I might have to rethink my earlier assessment. It's possible that Matthias is a long-tailed duck and not an *aqiggiit* after all.

And I confess that months later, when I sat down to write this account, I did consult the ornithological literature, but not to check on the accuracy of Matthias's arrival or departure dates or clutch size estimates. I checked multiple sources for the one important piece of information that I'd neglected to ask of him: the foundation or meaning of the Inuktitut name for long-tailed duck.

Aggiajuk.

I found no references. But with the two names printed before me, it hit me. Sounded out, *ag-gi-a-juk,* like *South southerly,* is a phonetic rendering of the bird's call. They're musical twins! Imagine that. The Inuit and Delaware waterman's cultures are joined at the ear by a bird that has a webbed foot in both camps.

Small world.

And listen, note to any of you coastal duck hunters whom I troubled with a call about a decade back. I have it on good authority that long-tailed ducks taste "very good." But it's possible you have to eat the bird between Nattian and Amiraijaut, when they are not in season for us nonaboriginal folk in the south (and not subsisting on a flesh-tainting diet of mollusks). I wouldn't invite friends for dinner until you've tested this possibility.

Nattian through Amiraijaut. Late June to early October. The time of Arctic Autumn.

CHAPTER 2

Moon Month of Mannitt (June–July), "Eggs"

Fourth of July Parade

Kongakut River, Arctic National Wildlife Refuge

The first breakfast of our Kongakut River raft trip—blueberry pancakes drenched in maple syrup with rivulets of butter running down the sides—was over. As individuals and couples, depending upon filial association and biological necessity, our group dispersed to organize gear and attend to other pressing matters.

Bob and Lisa, proprietors of Wilderness Birding Adventures, had decided not to start our party downriver as scheduled. Since weather and river conditions are never certain, there is a measure of flextime built into wilderness trips.

There is also something about being under the spell of Arctic Time that is poisonous to hurry and haste.

Our bush pilot had assured us that no other parties were scheduled to use the landing strip on Drain Creek. So taking advantage of this, and the fine weather, the decision was made to spend our first full day in the Arctic National Wildlife Refuge right where we were, exploring the North Slope of the Brooks Range—the northernmost mountain range on Earth.

"What are you going to put on your feet?" I asked my outdoor-savvy wife.

"Hiking boots. Why?"

"Well, I thought I'd wear wellies."

"Hiking boots will give you better support for climbing."

"Wellies will offer better protection if we hit any wet areas."

"Well, I'm wearing hiking boots. You can do what you want."

"Well, I'm wearing wellies. I don't want to get my hiking boots soaked early in the trip."

If this conversation sounds practiced, that's because it is. What to put on your feet is the biggest question in the Arctic, and every answer seems wrong. If you go with hiking boots, it is guaranteed that you are going to find a sodden patch of tundra to slog through (and your boots will stay wet for the duration). If you don knee-high rubber boots, it is equally certain that your route will intersect a scree-paved slope whose weather-napped elements will shred the uppers from the soles and ensure that, for the rest of the trip, your feet will be as wet as everyone else's.

One thing we didn't have to worry about was snow. On this date, at this latitude (and this year), summer reigned.

Despite debate and indecision, Linda and I were ready

to travel before the rest of the group. We started on ahead, climbing the knoll across the creek for the view and whatever surprises the wilderness had in store for us this beautiful Fourth of July morning.

Ten minutes later we were above the camp, watching clouds flirt with mountaintops still under construction. The view alone was worth the price of admission, which is, as ten-day raft trips in the Arctic tend to be, not inconsiderable.

Flanked by walls of stone, still bracketed here and there by ice, the Kongakut River churned its way toward the waters of the Beaufort Sea. One of the more tranquil rivers flowing north out of the Brooks, the Kongakut is generally less popular than other waterways, most notably the Noatak and Sheenjek. Chances were our group would have the river to ourselves for the duration of the float.

Which was perfect. In fact, it was priceless. There are, now, in this age of the hairless plains ape, so few places where a person can go to interface with wilderness in solitude. If the appeal of this escapes you, consider the words of a celebrated nineteenth-century traveler: "It is difficult to imagine the charm surrounding these pretty places where man has not erected his dwellings and where a deep peace and uninterrupted silence still reign."

The wilderness admirer's name was Alexis de Tocqueville. His observations about America and Americans, compiled in 1831, have been quoted by every American president since Dwight David Eisenhower, and his book, *Democracy in America*, has been called, among other accolades, a "mirror to Americans."

"Boo," said Linda.

"Wrong holiday," I corrected. "You're jumping way ahead."

"What are you talking about?"

"The Fourth of July. Independence Day. 'Boo' goes with Halloween, and that's four months away. Brass bands, bunting, and parades go with the Fourth and that's today. What are you talking about?"

"I'm talking about *Boo*," she said, treating me to one of those flat-mouthed, head-shaking looks that wives direct at exasperating, oblique-minded husbands. "Like that bunch heading our way right now," she added, pointing.

"Oooh," I said, bringing my binoculars up, focusing them on the string of big, brown, long-legged ungulates that had materialized at the head of the creek. "Caribou!"

There were thirteen animals in all. Cows and young bulls along with a single calf—members of the Porcupine caribou herd. After spending most of their year in the Yukon, every spring the herd crosses into the United States, where females drop their calves in the foothills of the northern Brooks and adjacent coastal plain. In late June, they head back toward the Yukon.

Yesterday, on our flight in, we'd overflown about fifteen hundred animals in groups ranging from a dozen to more than four hundred. Squeezed by mountain passes or spread across trail-scoured slopes, the animals were on the move. It is the migration that has earned the Arctic Coastal Plain the nickname the "Serengeti of the North." It is also the first major migratory event of Arctic Autumn.

"Oh noooo," Linda moaned, "they are going to walk right through camp!"

It seemed that the first surprise the wilderness had in store for us was to cheat Linda out of a photo op.

"We should alert . . . ," I started, but my tribal inclinations were moot. Our fellow Americans had already seen the advancing column and were mustering to engage. Rushing to the banks of the creek down which the animals seemed determined to pass. Eager smiles on flanking faces. Cameras poised in waiting hands. Necks craned, as viewers tried to gauge the progress of the lead animal.

"It looks like people lining up for the Fourth of July parade," Linda observed, laughing, and indeed it did—eight eager, camera-toting Americans enjoying the pageantry commemorating America's most patriotic holiday.

The composition of this parade was different. Instead of fire engines, antique cars, and the local scout troop carrying flags, the sole entertainment would be a troop of tundra deer. But the anticipation shining in the eyes of those along the parade route equaled, and maybe eclipsed, any found along parade routes elsewhere across the United States.

Among our troop of parade watchers was Tony, an affable San Francisco art dealer with earnest eyes, a short-clipped beard, and a voice that hesitates between a rumble and a purr. Next to him was his tent mate and the recently retired Alaska director of the Wilderness Society, Alan Smith. Hidden behind his ruddy, sourdough caricature of a face was a restless mind and an earnest love of the Arctic his efforts had helped preserve.

Standing next to them were Ned and Diane—sometime residents on their ranch in Idaho, sometime residents on their five-hundred-acre farm in Virginia, as often as they can be backcountry, horse-packing conservationists. Ned is a lean, reserved philanthropist with an honest laugh and a patrician bearing; Diane, an intelligent, dark-haired, soft-voiced sculptor. What scant wrinkles might be found on her youthful face are the tracks left by a lifetime of smiles.

Standing next to them, as bubbly and enthusiastic as a Girl Scout troop leader, was Jeannie. Short and blond, given to smiles and quips, she works as marketing manager for an engineering firm in Anchorage but lives, three days a week, in Homer with her husband, George. A retired Alaskan civil servant, past president of Anchorage Audubon Society, former member of the Alaska Board of Game, and full-time conservationist, George and his sixty-nine years fit comfortably into a lean, tan, fifty-year-old's body—one that has visited the Arctic many times.

Last and certainly not least, Bob Dittrick and Lisa Moorehead, founders of Wilderness Birding Adventures—our trip organizers (and longtime friends). If the names Bob and Lisa sound familiar, then you are the careful sort of reader whose attentiveness to detail includes noting the dedications in books.

That was our group. Eight red-blooded Americans—ten, including Linda and me. The youngest among us fifty, the oldest sixty-nine. Some hailing from the East, some from the West. Some were Republicans, some Democrats. All of us were approaching, or enjoying, the autumn of our lives. All of us were products of the "American Dream" and had enjoyed successful lives growing up in the postwar United States.

And all of us were celebrating Independence Day on the banks of the Kongakut River, in the Alaskan wilderness, instead of attending family picnics, small-town parades, concerts in the park, and fireworks displays like every other red-blooded Dick, Jane, and Sally were doing.

A good question for you to ask right now would be . . .

Why?

In 1831, when the ambitious twenty-five-year-old French aristocrat Alexis de Tocqueville embarked upon his nine-month journey across the United States of America, he was driven by curiosity about this strange experiment in democracy and a fascination with what amounted to a whole new social offshoot of humankind. These were the American people.

It was a nation and people set free from the hobbling class distinctions of Europe. One characterized by boundless, almost frenetic, drive and energy. One in which the right of "self-determination" was a priori; "individualism" was not just respected but revered; and the acquisition of material wealth was the ambition that fueled the whole shooting match.

But if there is a single American trait that fascinates Europeans, then and now, it is the boundless optimism that Americans bring to bear upon their world.

Where does this sense of optimism spring from? Living in the land of opportunity, of course.

What is the source of opportunity? Nature. Open, unbridled wilderness—and I am not referring merely to physical resources, like timber and minerals. I'm talking about a people whose thinking was shaped, and whose ambitions nurtured, by an environment whose physical boundaries were not even known in 1831.

So not just the land of opportunity. A land of *unlimited* opportunity!

Maybe a less resourceful people would have regarded the wilderness as a barrier. But to Americans, the virgin land lying to the west was part destiny, part sign of the covenant, all there for the taking. During de Tocqueville's time, a flood of Americans were leaving their foothold on the eastern seaboard; cutting their way into climax forests and turning sod on the eastern edge of the prairie—changing the character of both.

When I was growing up in Whippany, New Jersey, I used to dream of heading into the wilderness, living off the land. These red-blooded ambitions were most acute the evening before some school assignment (which I'd ignored for three weeks) was due or after engaging in one of those challenging exchanges that marked my public school years.

"Now class, if a equals b and b equals c . . ."

"That's impossible."

"Mr. Dunne, do you have something to share with the class?"

"I said that's impossible. A doesn't equal b. They're different letters."

"It's how theorems are expressed in algebra, by using letters instead of numbers."

"Well, then, algebra is really stupid. If two things are different, they can't be the same. Just saying they're the same doesn't make them the same."

"Mr. Dunne, you will see me after class, please."

Anyway, during moments of soul-searching, I used to retreat into my wilderness fantasy. Imagine the day (coming soon) when I'd put a frame pack on my back. Whistle for my fictional dog, Rex. Grab the lever-action, .30-30 rifle that rested (in my dreams) over my bed and, cradling it, Daniel Boone fashion, in the crook of m'arm, set off into the wilderness, never to return.

Until, after a successful career as a pioneer, explorer, gold miner, trapper, and discoverer of six or nine mountain ranges, I'd show up in class and impress all those stupid, brainwashed future accountants, engineers, and regional salesmen with what a real American with gumption could do when he stopped listening to this a equals b equals c crap.

In the end, I never did muster the requisite gumption. But I did have the dream.

De Tocqueville's study of Americans, their means of governance, and their character, was summarized in his two-volume treatise, *Democracy in America*. Published in 1835 and 1840, the work still ranks among the most insightful and quoted books of all time. Much of what he said about Americans then rings true today.

Less heralded than his social and political probings was the two-week trip the then-twenty-six-year-old de Tocqueville made into the American wilderness, a journey that took him through old-growth forests that did not survive the century to the banks of the Saginaw River, on the edge of the American prairie and through what is now Michigan, Wisconsin, and southern Canada. The essay recounting his wilderness journey, "Two Weeks in the Wilderness," was published after his death and not even translated into English until the twentieth century.

Why would a man, traveling on a tight budget and with the objective of understanding a people, take a two-week side trip into the wilderness beyond the farthest advances of his subject? Just one reason I can imagine. De Tocqueville knew that the only way to understand Americans was to understand the wilderness that shaped them.

The European visitor was impressed by the restless energy

of the American people. He admired their industrious nature. He was fascinated by what he saw as America's fixation on making money. He was awed by its wilderness and, having correctly assessed the frenetic, industrious, money-driven focus of the American juggernaut, not optimistic about the future of wilderness in America.

"After not many years, these impassible forests will be felled," he lamented. "The din of civilization and industry will break the silence. . . . The idea of this natural and wild grandeur, which will come to an end, blends with the imperious images evoked by the triumphant progress of civilization."

De Tocqueville was right about many things. And he was downright prescient with regard to the future of wilderness in America. Over the course of the next two hundred years, the wilderness was converted into farms and ranches and cities and towns. The people who were responsible for the "triumphant progress of civilization" grew to long for the "deep peace and uninterrupted silence" they had known when the land was opportunity instead of wealth and property.

The ache is still here, passed on to us, the heirs of pioneers. The restlessness, too. But the wilderness, largely, is not. It had been pushed back into the most remote corners of the continent, far from the people it shaped and inspired who were, today, standing alongside main streets in small towns all across America.

Most of them, anyway.

CHANGE OF ROUTE
The lead cow in the parade halted about seventy-five yards short of camp. Lead animals don't assume that position by accident, or even by the democratic process. De Tocqueville

correctly assessed that uniformity and conformity of thinking constitute democracy's greatest weakness, and he believed that these qualities promote mediocrity in leadership. This affliction is not shared by caribou. As among Inuit, it is experience and judgment, not public opinion or majority rule, that get an animal to the head of the line.

The lead animal had certainly seen people before. Recognized them as a potential threat. Assessed that the planned route would bring her and the group uncomfortably close to the gathering. She elected to skirt the crowd and take a route that would carry them a little farther from our gathered companions but, as it turned out, closer to Linda and me.

Then, with hooves clicking and heads held parade-ground high, the animals kicked off. Clydesdales of the North, drawing a wagon brimming with wild America behind. Passing marvelously close. Being admired and photographed as they passed. The finest, most unique Fourth of July parade in these fifty states.

Earlier in this chapter, I posed a question. Asked why it was that ten Americans would invoke their right of self-determination and miss the July Fourth holiday at home to stand on the banks of an obscure river in the Arctic National Wildlife Refuge.

The answer is that we weren't missing the holiday at all. In fact, I would argue that, even more than all those other Americans in small towns across the United States, we were celebrating it in style.

Ten Americans. Shareholders in the American Dream who had made their mark and their money but were still driven to go all the way to the frontier to fill some ambition yet unsatisfied by the acquisition of material things, which de Tocqueville saw as the cornerstone of American ambition.

Something that even the most vested and patriotic American still longs for.

Something that has been compromised and diminished along the way—space, peace, freedom.

The real question isn't why ten Americans were watching their Fourth of July parade from the banks of the Kongakut. The question is who are the real Americans?

The ten people still searching, still pushing, still finding themselves and values affirmed by wilderness today? Or the millions passively standing along parade routes, paying homage to "Old Glory"?

The thirteen caribou, one for each of the original colonies, splashed across the river and continued on. There was no applause, no cheers, no flag waving from the crowd. Just smiles and the heartfelt thanks of a grateful people.

CHAPTER 3

Moon Month of Mannitt (late June–July), "Eggs"

Oil and Feathers Don't Mix

Teshekpuk Lake, National Petroleum Reserve, Alaska

This is amazing, I thought, and might have said, but it's un-likely anyone aboard our single-engine Otter would have heard it.

Not our young pilot, who was chatting by radio with the next client on his work sheet. Not Bob Dittrick, who was peering out the copilot's window, trying to juxtapose topographic features one thousand feet below with the ponds and rivers outlined on the deck of downloaded maps sitting on his lap.

Not Linda, who was busy shooting images of the Arctic Coastal Plain and Beaufort Sea beyond; nor the two young biologists, wedged in with our gear, who had bummed a ride out of Deadhorse to conduct breeding bird surveys at Lonely.

Lonely, by the way, is a place, not a state of mind.

The Otter, the Clydesdale of bush-flying aircraft, is one noisy piece of machinery. Even without the sound-dampening plugs wedged into our ears, utterances spoken with less volume than a shout commonly went unheard.

"Absolutely amazing," I said or thought again, looking down at the green-brown carpet below that was tundra, and the overlying grid of pipes, petroleum transfer stations, and service roads that constitute the oil production fields of Prudhoe Bay on Alaska's North Slope—the source of about 6 percent of the petroleum produced in the United States, not to mention the annual dividend check given to every Alaskan resident.

You thought I was marveling at some extraordinary natural spectacle, didn't you? No. I was referring to the colossal oil-extracting infrastructure, now more than thirty years in the making, that mantles the coastal plain west of Deadhorse, "Oil City," Alaska. We'd been in the air almost forty minutes, and the capillary network of roads and pipes feeding the Trans Alaska Pipeline still dominated the landscape below.

It looked as if the tundra had been turned into a giant computer circuit board. It represented the work of tens of thousands of workers and billions of dollars and was incontrovertible evidence supporting not only the profitability of oil but the world's dependence upon this energy-infused liquid as well.

No single engineering ambition that I have ever seen or read about compares with the transformed landscape below.

Not the road system of Ancient Rome. Not the Suez Canal or the Great Wall of China. As the miles fell behind, as the scope of this landscape-altering endeavor unfolded below, these and other totems of human achievement diminished in significance and scale.

Am I castigating the oil industry? Hell no. How could anybody who grew up in a home heated with fuel oil, who commutes forty miles a day to and from work, and who was at that very moment ferrying himself and two accomplices, plus their 650 pounds of gear, out to a remote airstrip on the Beaufort Sea aboard a plane that is hardly known for its fuel efficiency possibly chastise the industry that I support (and depend upon) every time I pull up to the pump?

All I am doing is honestly acknowledging one of human civilization's greatest feats of imagination, determination, and engineering. No other species could have come to one of the most remote and inhospitable corners of the world and so completely suborned such an ambition-defying landscape. If it was my privilege to award a medal to the single greatest engineering feat of the twentieth century, it wouldn't be manned space flight, it would not be the telecommunications network, it would be Prudhoe Bay.

"We are an amazing species," I thought or said to myself as we overflew the last of the pump relay stations and our plane approached the braided mudscape that is the Colville River Delta. The land below went from being a green-brown circuit board to being a green-brown polygonal landscape sparkling with lakes and ponds; most thawed, some still garnished with a core of winter ice; many supporting clustered flocks of waterfowl.

It is this preponderance of lakes, combined with the region's untroubled remoteness and with the surfeit of nutrient-rich vegetation, that has made the Teshekpuk Lake region of Alaska's Arctic Coastal Plain the sanctuary of choice for tens of thousands of geese during their post-breeding molt.

The problem is it's not a sanctuary. While outside the boundary of the Prudhoe Bay Oil Field, the area we hoped to explore was nevertheless part of the 23.5-million-acre National Petroleum Reserve—the nation's single largest publicly owned block of land. It was set aside by President Warren Harding in 1923 to meet the anticipated future fuel needs of what was, then, a petroleum-fueled navy, and, in 1976, jurisdiction was transferred by Congress to the Department of the Interior. During the Reagan administration, Congress authorized oil and gas leasing and development here.

But one portion of the reserve was still deemed too environmentally sensitive to allow development. This was the 1,734,000-acre Teshekpuk Lake Special Area, lying directly east of and adjacent to the oil fields of Prudhoe Bay. This environmentally sensitive area had already been whittled down by successive administrations to a core of 588,998 acres representing the very heart of the waterfowl molting and caribou calving grounds when, in January 2006, the U.S. Department of the Interior, under pressure from the George W. Bush administration, authorized oil and gas drilling. A coalition of environmental groups challenged the decision, and, in September 2006, the U.S. District Court for Alaska put lease efforts on hold pending additional public comment.

Our visit, in July 2007, put us smack in the middle of disputed wetlands and the controversy—between those who wanted to open the area to oil drilling and those who regard it as too biologically significant.

It is the story of the Arctic in a nutshell. Isolation versus intrusion, protection versus exploitation.

An hour later, with our pilot once again in the air and our hip-boot-shod biologist friends slogging south, Bob, Linda, and I were on the ground, sorting out gear beside the well-maintained gravel runway that once served Lonely, one of the network of DEW line radar sites that kept their watchful electronic eyes trained on the skies over the Arctic Icecap—Canada's and the United States's first line of defense against a Soviet transpolar attack.

Decommissioned at the end of the Cold War, the radar towers now serve as nest sites for ravens and rough-legged hawks; the abandoned and weathering buildings are infested with snow buntings who take to them the way bluebirds take to nest boxes.

"Been a while since I've put together one of these things," Bob said, nodding toward the garbage-can-size sack containing the elements of our folding canoe.

"Unless that pack ice moves offshore, we're not going to need to test your memory," Linda said, nodding in the direction of the Beaufort Sea, the body of water that defines Alaska's northern coast.

"Noticed that, huh?" Bob said, smiling even more broadly.

"Better than loading our boats, getting twenty miles away, and then having the ice come in and pin us to the beach," I observed.

"Well," said Bob. "You guys said you wanted an adventure. And there's still plenty of time for that to happen, too." This time he wasn't smiling.

We pitched our tents on an invitingly flat stretch of tundra east of the runway. It wasn't until the next morning that we realized the chosen substrate had once supported the fuel pipe running from the beach to the half dozen massive fuel tanks that served the radar station.

It takes a lot of oil to keep a string of prefab buildings warm when temperatures drop to forty and fifty below zero.

Further deduction led to the conclusion that the Dumpster-size, gravel-filled plastic bags stacked beside the runway were probably put there by the HAZMAT cleanup teams ordered in after base personnel were ordered out.

Did I mention that Lonely is a Superfund site? And if you are wondering why two residents of New Jersey would fly all the way to the Arctic to camp in a Superfund site (when we have, in our petroleum-refinery-rich corner of the planet, so many perfectly fine Superfund sites closer to home), read on.

SOMEPLACE YOU HAVE NEVER BEEN . . .

"Is there anyplace you've never been above the Arctic Circle?" I'd asked Bob way back when Linda and I were planning our adventure. "Someplace you've always wanted to go but couldn't justify because you knew you couldn't sell a trip or it was too expensive?"

There was a thoughtful silence over the phone while our friend pondered the question. Bob has been an Alaska resident for over thirty years and organizing backpacking, rafting, and kayaking trips for more than twenty of them. While Alaska is a big and spectacle-rich state, places Bob has not explored are getting harder to find.

Linda and I have done close to a dozen trips with Bob and his wife, Lisa. Backpacked out of the Brooks Range; rafted, kayaked, or canoed the Kongakut, Canning, Colville, and Pilgrim rivers. Sometimes as paying clients (at our insistence), other times as co-paying partners in trips organized for adventure and friends.

They know what they are doing, they know their state, and they've got great judgment and are able to make good risk assessments, on the spot, when things don't go according to plan (and this is not the exception in wilderness travel).

"How about Teshekpuk," Bob suggested. "It's been in the news a lot lately. Bush wants to open it up to oil exploration, but it is a critical molting area for black brant and other geese. Even James Watt declared the area too sensitive for drilling," he added, "and you know how environmentally sensitive he was."

James Watt, a secretary of the interior under Ronald Reagan, was, during his tenure, pretty close to the environmental Antichrist in the circles I traveled in. For even Watt to close the area to oil exploration underscored an environmental significance.

"Ever since the decision was made to open Teshekpuk up in 2006, I've been thinking about getting up there and seeing it," Bob explained.

"Never heard of it," I confessed. "Is it near the Arctic National Wildlife Refuge?"

"No," he confided. "It's west of Prudhoe. In the National Petroleum Reserve."

"Do we get there via the Colville?" I asked, trying to salvage a bit of dignity by indicating I knew that the largest river on the North Slope constitutes the southern and eastern boundary of the reserve.

"No," he said. "It's just in from the Beaufort Sea. We'll have to fly in out of Barrow or Deadhorse, I guess. If that sounds like fun to you, I can do some investigation and find out when we'll need to be there to see a bunch of geese near some landing strip. We'll need permits, of course."

It sounded like a fine plan. And it was mostly after Bob and Lisa's busy rafting season. And as subjects go, it was smack on—an early-season biological marker demonstrating the rapidity of autumn in the Arctic. Breeding finished, bam! Time for geese to molt in new flight suits for the long journey south.

Plus, it incorporated the element of oil exploration and extraction—an unavoidable subject in the Arctic these days.

I had no idea that the trip would ultimately also incorporate elements of the Cold War and global warming. I further had no idea that our plan would be deemed so controversial that an effort would be made to prevent us from going.

By the oil companies? No. By people who care as much about birds and wildlife as Linda, Bob, and I do.

By a friend.

OUR MAN IN FAIRBANKS

Ted Swem, of the U.S. Fish and Wildlife Service, is a tall, curly-haired career biologist known for his puckish wit, uncommon intelligence, lateral thinking, dedication, knowledge, and outstanding margaritas.

He and Bob have been friends for decades. In fact, I met both of them at the same time: in Cape May, New Jersey, in 1976, when the three of us became colleagues and housemates in the inaugural year of the Cape May Bird Observatory. There weren't a lot of margaritas consumed that year. We were, all of us, rat-poor journeymen raptor fanatics with lives and careers still ahead of us. Bob's path led him to design and oversee natural history interpretation projects for the State of Alaska. I went on to become the director of the Cape May Bird Observatory. Ted joined the Fish and Wildlife Service, working in their Fairbanks office, where he now rides herd upon Alaska's federally endangered species.

We've known each other a long time. Our respect for each other is immense. So Lisa's e-mail advising us that Ted was strongly opposed to our trip was as much of a surprise as it was a matter of concern. Ted's objection stemmed from the heightened sensitivity exhibited by geese during their molt. Any intrusion, he argued, was an unwarranted intrusion. The mere glimpse of a person coming over the horizon, according to Ted, was enough to send the birds charging across the tundra.

Note I said "charging," not "flying," and this distinction is central to the discussion.

The way most birds, most commonly, deal with a perceived threat is to fly away from it. As defensive strategies go, flying rates an evolutionary 9.5 but not a perfect 10.

A bird's ability to fly is contingent upon a number of morphological refinements, all working in concert. These include a weight-reducing hollow superstructure, a superrich fuel mixture, a high-volume air-intake system, and a large muscular power train.

But key to this concept and design is a revolutionarily honed device called a "feather." Basically superrefined scales that hark back to the reptilian ancestry of birds, feathers are marvelously light, marvelously strong, and multifunctional. They keep birds warm and dry, make them attractive or hard to see, and, best of all, some of these feathers are further refined to serve as airfoils. Laid in an overlapping plane along the length of a bird's wing, they confer the ability to fly.

The problem is, feathers wear out. Flight feathers, especially for those species that fly habitually or migrate long distances, must be replaced, or molted, every year.

There are two ways in which birds accomplish this, two strategies. Some birds, like birds of prey, molt their important flight feathers gradually and synchronously—in other words, two at a time, same feather on each wing. It's a little like overhauling an old sports car two parts at a time. The car's always drivable. But, as with most old sports cars, repairs are never finished, and the car never looks or runs the way it did right out of the showroom.

The other strategy is to just do all the body work at once. Drop the old feathers and replace them with new ones over the course of several weeks. It means walking and swimming are going to take the place of flight for as long as the job takes (for most species a month or more). But it means that, once the molt is over, you're back in tiptop form again. Able to fly great distances and escape predators with right-out-of-the-showroom ease.

For geese, the total overhaul (or complete molt) strategy makes good energetic and evolutionary sense. The time they choose to conduct their molt is biological downtime. Post-breeding, pre-migration. In the Arctic, this means late June into early August.

As birds that swim as well as walk, they are ambulatory enough to forage and escape most forms of danger.

What they require to make the strategy really work is a place that meets their needs while they are in the shop. Someplace where food is abundant, so they won't have to travel far, and highly nutritious, because growing feathers requires quality material and energy conservation.

Most of all, the birds need security, a place where predators are few and intrusion minimal. Energy consumed avoiding a potential danger means less time feeding, and this translates to more downtime in the shop.

The area north and east of Teshekpuk meets and exceeds the requirements of molting geese. Two highly nutritional salt-tolerant plants, Hoppner's sedge and creeping alkaligrass, thrive in the region's marshes. The multitude of large lakes provide a safe retreat to rest and roost. The relative scarcity of predators (including and, perhaps, most notably, humans) reduces risk while birds are most vulnerable.

Small wonder that as many as thirty-seven thousand brant (about one third of the West Coast population) and approximately thirty-five thousand greater white-fronted geese, whose next stop will be the Gulf Coastal states and Mexico, choose the Teshekpuk Lake Special Area to molt.

The region's wealth of birds, and their sensitivity, has been recognized for decades. It is what prompted three secretaries of the interior—Cecil Andrus in 1977, James Watt in 1983, and Bruce Babbitt in 1998—to declare the most critical molting areas of the area off-limits to drilling.

It is also why Ted Swem was so concerned about our plans to go there. He polled two other biologists—but got a split decision. One agreed with Ted; one thought the impact would be minimal. The matter was ameliorated, if not settled, by outside arbitration. Lisa and Bob sought the counsel of Stan Senner, director of Audubon Alaska, who was, then, at the center of the legal efforts to reverse the decision to sell drilling permits in the Teshekpuk region. Stan did not consider our trip abusively intrusive. In fact, he was supportive of skilled outside observers going to the area and commenting on what they saw.

Me? I thought Ted was overreacting and maybe falling victim to the entitlement syndrome that occasionally grips researchers—i.e., that the intrusion visited upon wildlife by people doing research is sanctionable while intrusion by visitors and viewers (who gather impressions, not data) is not.

I was also confident that three more conscientious, wildlife-sensitive people than Linda, Bob, and myself could not possibly be found. Zero impact is an ethic Bob, and Wilderness Birding Adventures, champions. It was the ethic Linda taught at National Outdoor Leadership School.

And, heck, I work for the New Jersey Audubon Society! Ensuring the safety and integrity of birds and bird populations is what I do for a living. I've engaged lots of molting waterfowl in my time. I couldn't see how anything we planned would disrupt the Teshekpuk birds in any way.

We weren't dismissive of Ted's arguments. In fact, we were even more sensitive to the geese, and their need for privacy, than we might ordinarily have been.

But we were also not dissuaded.

LONELY MISGIVINGS

We woke that first morning at Lonely to the chatter of red-necked phalarope and the croaking of red-throated loon—a sound a bird might make if it were trying to sneeze and cough simultaneously.

Ra rah ra'harh

The ice-chilled winds, which had been moving thirty-four-degree air over our site the day before, had turned and moderated. Overnight, temperatures had climbed to a very comfortable forty-five degrees Fahrenheit.

Make that "while we slept." There is no night at this latitude, in early July, because the sun never sets.

The offshore winds had also pushed the ice pack out to sea, opening a path for us. Our plan was to head east, hugging the coast, about twelve air miles, then nose our two-craft flotilla into a channel that, according to our topo maps, would carry us deep into the marshy lake region. Fish and Wildlife survey maps, secured by Bob, showed the area rife with molting birds—with brant numbers alone ranging up to seven-thousand on assorted lakes.

We did not plan to actually reach Teshekpuk Lake. The "Big Coastal Lake" as it translates from the Inupiat language, was still frozen and would remain so well into July. It was the area north and east of the lake that was the principal molting area. And waterfowl are not the only animals drawn to the solitude and security offered by the region.

"Olhmlyglod," Linda managed to say through a mouthful of masticated cold cereal.

Five bull caribou went prancing by our camp, crossed the runway, and disappeared behind the gravel embankment. Linda's reflexive reach for her camera was about an expletive slow.

"Hand me your binoculars, will'ya," Bob encouraged. He trained the instrument on the horizon, the magnified image confirming what his eyes had detected and distance had tried to conceal.

"Lots of them out there," he said. And there were. Fifty or sixty animals grazing just beyond the old radar installation; another twenty-five hundred moving like a pale brown tide along the distant horizon. Only a fraction of the forty-five thousand animals estimated to be in the Teshekpuk Lake herd but not a bad down payment on this, our first full day at Lonely.

If the camel is the ship of the desert, then the caribou is the ship of the Arctic. There are many differences between these two ungulates, but one thing they very much have in common. Both animals are superbly designed for their environments.

Caribou, *Rangifer tarandus*, is a member of the deer family whose other North American representatives include moose, elk, and white-tailed and mule deer. Falling between deer and moose in size, they are considered conspecific with the reindeer of Eurasia.

Their bodies are short and stocky to conserve body heat. Their legs are long to help the animals move through deep snow, and their long, dense coats protect the animals from winter cold (and summer insects). Unlike other North American ungulates, both males and females have antlers.

Impressive? Absolutely. Attractive? Not particularly. In fact, their short-muzzled faces (another adaptation to cold environments) give the animals a mulelike character. But what they lack in terms of one-on-one winsomeness, they more than make up for in numbers, because caribou are the most numerous large mammal of the Arctic.

Split into four subspecies, divided into multiple herds, more than 3 million caribou range across the North American Arctic and adjacent boreal forest. The most nomadic of these are the Barren Ground caribou, whose annual peregrinations may cover thousands of miles. In winter, the great herds retreat into the northern edge of the boreal forest. In early spring, with snow still deep on the ground, they range onto open tundra, where females drop their calves. The migrations to and from the breeding grounds are among the most celebrated animal movements on the planet.

Many of the Arctic's aboriginal people molded their movements and cultures around caribou, becoming nomads who followed the herds. Arctic wolves are virtually caribou obligates, and in some regions breeding success, or failure, hinges upon the capricious wanderings of the herds. No book treating the Arctic is complete without discussion of this animal, and no photographer visiting the Arctic does not dream of being surrounded by streams of these rack-bearing ungulates.

Having missed her shot, Linda started scanning the horizon, picking up small bands and studying their routes.

I knew what she was thinking. Better caribou in the hand than brant in the bush. Wildlife photographers learn to strike while the iron is hot. The most expensive and sophisticated cameras on earth don't come with temporal adjustment settings. You can't set them forward to capture tomorrow's great images; you can't set them back to nail the caribou that just ran by. If caribou is the hand the Arctic is dealing today, then caribou, at close range, in gorgeous sunlight is what 500-millimeter lenses (and photographers) should be focusing on *right now!*

But today was a travel day. And the Arctic is as parsimonious with good travel days as she is with great photo ops. If we wanted to get to the birds, which were the focus of our trip, the caribou would have to wait.

It took the better part of the morning to bang the boats together. Several more hours to apportion and load our gear.

Subsequent days would go more quickly, easily. There would be ample time to study and savor the many birds and animals that we were, by necessity, forced to turn a blind eye (and capped lens) to, today.

At lunch, six more caribou ambled by, down the beach, heads high, antlers back, eyes wide, and expressions semi-crazed. An hour later we were in our boats, paddling east. Five hours later, arms aching, and not particularly encouraged by the condition of the shore ahead, we decided to make camp on a bluff designated by the name Kokruagarok on Bob's map. We'd traveled slightly less than four miles, making not even one mile per hour.

No, the ice conditions were fine. It was the tide, the waves, and the headwinds that killed us.

MELTDOWN I

We headed for the Kokruagarok bluffs and the quarter-moon-shaped gravel beach, encouraged by the prospect of landing, getting out of the boats, and uncramping our legs. Five hours is a long time to sit with your legs contoured around gear. The snap-down cover on our canoe, intended, literally, to make the craft "seaworthy" (i.e., able to shed waves in open water), wasn't designed with long-legged fifty-six-year-old bird watchers in mind.

Or, more specifically, goose watchers.

"Aren't those geese ahead of us?" Linda directed.

I trained my binoculars on the animate mass of birds hauling themselves out of the water and onto the beach.

"Brant?" she asked.

"No . . . Canadas I think. *Hey, Bob, geese on the beach.*"

Bob, slightly ahead and more than slightly hard of hearing (for this Ted Nugent and the Rolling Stones, played at cranked amplification, share equal credit), didn't hear me, but he'd seen the birds, too.

About two hundred molting Canada geese, judging by their massed ranks and coordinated movement, had suddenly elected to find a less contested place. What this means is that the birds were charging up the bank.

"We're still five hundred yards from shore," I gauged. "They can't be reacting to us."

And I cannot say, with absolute certainty, that the birds *were* reacting to our appearance. Or that the beach, which was covered in nodular goose droppings and shed feathers, both old and new, was a favorite lounging area for molting birds (so one that they would be disinclined to abandon). All I can tell you, empirically speaking, is this:

That two hundred flightless geese very abruptly and for no (other) apparent reason suddenly vacated a favored beach by charging, en masse, up and over the hill.

That after landing, when we climbed to the top of the hill and scanned around, they (or another flock numbering two hundred Canada geese) were about a mile away and still running in a direction that led directly away from us.

That for the thirteen hours we remained on that stretch of beach, the birds never returned, and none of the groups of birds flying and swimming past took their place.

What I can say is that, at that point, a little voice inside my head whispered this possibility: Ted was right. Molting geese are off-the-chart spooky here.

On the other hand, for the pair of Arctic foxes whose den

was on the bluff, not only was retreat not an option but it seemed not even to be on their minds. Nor, for that matter, was it on the mind of the greater white-fronted goose who was incubating her clutch of eggs beside a small pond not far from where we pitched our tents.

In fact, neither the foxes—one piebald animal, one black one—nor the geese paid much attention to us at all. They were much more fixated on each other and the eggs that were at stake. The nonchalance of many Arctic birds and mammals in the face of human intrusion is something I have marveled at on previous visits. It made the reaction of the geese even more startling and dramatic.

I figured my photographer wife would be delighted by the proximity of animals, but I was wrong.

"You could probably get some good shots of those foxes," I encouraged Linda, who was facing away and, curiously, in the process of stowing her camera gear.

"I tried," she said, to her pack, not me. "The fog came in and the light's gone."

I don't know how I knew she was crying, but I did. And I was almost as perplexed by this as I was by the retreat of the geese.

"What's the matter?" I asked in the tone that husbands use upon discovering that their wives are upset by something that has completely escaped their notice.

"Are you upset because we spooked the geese?"

She shook her head no.

"Don't you like the campsite?"

No, again.

There ensued one of those pregnant pauses during which

wives weigh the perennial alternatives—swallow your frustra-
tion or throw it out on the table—and husbands stare, un-
breathing and unblinking, at the swords that have suddenly
and unexpectedly appeared above their heads and wonder
about the tensile strength of a thread.

"I don't want this to be another trip where all we do is travel
and there's no time to photograph," she said, once again, to
her camera pack. Then she turned, and I noticed first the fog
that was beading on her hair and then the tear streaks down
both cheeks.

"I know this chapter is about geese, but I could have had
some great shots of caribou this morning. This book involves
me, too, and I can't get any kind of shot if all we do is keep
moving around and chasing story lines."

She was right, of course. Writers are always pursuing story
lines, so want always to be on the move. Photographers need
time to set up shots, let the forces of the universe—light, angle, background, animation, proximity, perception, composition, and, of course, luck—come to bear. If we wanted good
photos, we couldn't keep running away from opportunities.

"It's only the second day," I soothed.

"I've seen the route. I know how far we traveled today. At
this rate, we'll be in our boats for the entire trip."

"We'll change the route," I said. "Take advantage of what we
see. Let's talk to Bob."

Which we did. And he agreed. But as things turned out, we
could easily have saved ourselves the discussion, because the
Arctic herself had decided to arbitrate the matter indepen-
dently. There were forces at play that would change not only
our timetable and route but the "story line" of this chapter

(not to mention the face of the planet). We got our first inkling of this script change the next morning.

MELTDOWN II

We got off early by Arctic standards (midmorning). The foxes were probably not unhappy to see us off. The greater white-fronted goose? Hard to say. Our presence may have daunted a predator or two.

We rounded the tip of Kokruagarok and came face-to-face with not only the expected headwind but a wall of ice.

No. Not the pack ice moving back onshore. It was the shore. The waters of the Beaufort Sea were lapping at a wall of ice. A fifteen-foot wall of permafrost exposed by wave action, the ice that underlies the Arctic, was naked to the sun. The overlying cap of tundra was coming off in peaty chunks, and water that had not been liquid for thousands of years was running in rivulets into the sea. The Arctic was disappearing in front of our eyes.

From a geologic standpoint, it would hardly be more shocking if the Sahara suddenly put forth springs or the Mediterranean Sea went dry. In fact, what is happening in the Arctic right now, as a result of climate change, will be far more consequential than either of these imagined comparisons. And while the changes will come first, and perhaps most dramatically, to the Arctic, they most certainly will not end here.

Still fighting a headwind, we made poor time, traveling less than three miles by lunch; we landed our boats on a tiny island that seemed not to appear on Bob's map.

"According to my GPS," he announced, "We're half a mile inland."

"So half a mile of coastline has disappeared since those GPS coordinates were logged?" I asked.

"Seems like," he said. "I also haven't seen too many places where we can land and camp. This coast is all blown out.

"You know," he added, "when we were flying in, I was having a hard time squaring what I could see from the air with my map. Now I know why. There've been a lot of changes."

Because of the wind, because of the lateness of the day, because of the uncertainty of the crossing ahead, we decided to turn south short of our destination, into Pogik Bay, reasoning that the islands at the mouth of the bay might have buffered the shore somewhat from erosion, hoping that we could locate some higher ground that would serve as a camp.

Fortunately, we did. We found an elevated berm about a mile from the mouth of the bay, which was being guarded by a male peregrine (who flew) and ten feet of peaty shoreline muck, much of which accompanied us to our campsite. It wasn't the most aesthetically pleasing wilderness campsite I've ever found. Surrounded, as it was, by rusting and half-buried fifty-five-gallon drums and the sun-rotted remains of the big white plastic X-marks-the-spot aircraft marker that notes the location of "U.S. Coast and Geodetic Survey Triangulation Station Bunny 1951."

But it *was* elevated. There were flat spots large enough to accommodate tents. The view of the bay and the surrounding flats was excellent. What's more, the sky, which had been overcast, was clearing. Best of all, the afternoon temperature had climbed to a balmy sixty degrees Fahrenheit and there were, as yet, no mosquitoes.

It was then that we decided to push no farther in our boats. Supporting this decision were the thousand or so brant and

Canada geese visible in the bay, bolstered by six yellow-billed loons, a snowy owl sitting on a distant hummock, and about ten thousand caribou moving along the horizon.

It looked like Linda might get a photo or two out of the deal after all.

The brant, our first sizable concentration, were about a half mile away and, while plainly aware of our intrusion, not panicked. The fact that they had a whole big bay to escape into probably had much to do with this, and, as we moved our gear to higher ground, they made use of that space by swimming, about a mile farther south.

It looked like shots of brant would not be among those photos.

THE DOUBLE WHAMMY—GEESE IN THE CROSSFIRE

When I envisioned a book about the Arctic, I truly hoped not to spill much ink on the subject of global warming. I'm not a climatologist. The Arctic is an anthology of stories waiting to be told—most of them more feel-good than climate change.

But like the phenomenon itself, there is no avoiding the subject. Just as its impact on the coast changed our plans and the focus of this chapter, its long-term effects seem destined to change the Arctic.

Still I am, even now, reluctant to completely change my original focus, which was to discuss the challenge presented by the need to meet our species' energy needs without undermining the wildlife resources we cherish. So I've decided to expand, more than shift, the discussion. To focus on the challenges posed by our species's dependence upon fossil fuels first from the front, then from the back end.

How the drilling for oil affects life in the Arctic. How the burning of it does, too. Beginning this discussion at the beginning or . . .

Have you ever wondered how all this oil got lodged under the Arctic in the first place? Even more fundamentally, have you ever wondered what oil is? Why it does what it does (including things we don't want it to do)?

Believe it or not, it begins with sunlight.

OH, SAY CAN YOU C

For many years I labored under the misapprehension that oil was essence of melted dinosaur. I trace this misconception to the 1964 New York World's Fair, where I was first exposed to the Sinclair Oil Corporation, whose Dinoland exhibit got top honors in my thirteen-year-old esteem, and whose company logo featured a large green brontosaurus.

Essence of dead dinosaur, and other large prehistoric animals, may figure in some small portion of the earth's petroleum deposits. But the bulk of this energy-packed syrup comes from a group of organisms found much lower on the food pyramid—in fact, just about at the bottom. Most of the earth's crude oil was at one time the algae and zooplankton that flourished in ancient lakes and seas. Mixed with and buried beneath sediment, transmuted by heat and pressure, the reconstituted detritus ultimately worked its way closer to the surface, where it waited for some clever creature to come along and release the magic trapped within it.

Energy. Forged in the bowels of the sun. The source of most of the energy found on Earth and a key element in the alchemy of almost all living things. Through an extraordinary process called "photosynthesis," plants are able to harvest inorganic carbon atoms from water (and air) and suborn the energy of sunlight to bind these carbon atoms in long, stable chains that are the building blocks of carbohydrates. The plants ultimately die, but the energy bound in the links of carbon chains survives, providing the chains' demise finds, or soon places them in, an anaerobic environment, like a silted seabed. Introduced to oxygen, the carbon atoms break their bonds to one another and link up with this attractive new element, forming, among other things, carbon dioxide.

The crude oil lying beneath Alaska's North Slope began as an amalgam of small living things, moving about in, then dying and falling into the sediment of, a shallow sea that covered northern Alaska hundreds of millions of years ago. Then, about 180 million years ago, the Pacific continental plate began overriding the American plate. One of the things this did was create the Brooks Range. Another thing it did was bury the ancient seabed, subjecting the organic slurry that had accumulated on the bottom to intense pressure and heat for millions of years. The result: about 25 billion barrels of energy-impregnated liquid trapped in pools lying beneath what would become, in time, a complex tundra biome known as the North Slope and the bottom of the Beaufort Sea.

Our species's use of oil as a source of light goes back mere hundreds of years and involves multiple civilizations. But it wasn't until the mid–nineteenth century, when the process of distilling it to make kerosene was discovered, that oil became an essential ingredient of "modern" life, first as a source of fuel for lamps (which was good news for whales, whose blubber was similarly rich in combustible carbon chains and who were being slaughtered to satisfy the human demand for oil). But it was the development and proliferation of the internal combustion engine that has fueled a demand for oil. A worldwide demand that has now reached 850 million barrels per day, with no slackening in sight.

A demand so great that recovering oil in places as remote and technically challenging as the Arctic is now well within economic reach. Places whose environmental integrity has, until now, been minimally affected by our species.

The ongoing extraction of oil from the earth is not, in itself, necessarily a problem for Arctic wildlife. Yes, there is the danger or leaks or spills (such as the March 2006 Alaska Pipeline rupture), but these are not common, which is good, because the damage caused by spills in the Arctic environment is difficult to redress. The greatest short-term threat to wildlife in general, and to the molting geese and calving caribou of the Teshekpuk in particular, is the impact of development—compounded disruptions posed by thousands of workers, multiple vehicles, and persistent air traffic going on for years. If the appearance of two small nonmotorized boats and their occupants can send geese stampeding for the horizon, imagine the impact on geese caused by steady air traffic and round-the-clock human activity at every compass point.

The other major problem is the long-term impact of dropping a man-made infrastructure atop a fragile, natural one. Natural, elevated structures that support the nests of cliff-nesting predators such as ravens and raptors are rare in the low, flat, treeless reaches of the coastal plain.

The cliffs flanking the Colville River, more than a hundred miles to the south, support one of the highest densities of nesting raptors in the Arctic—golden eagles, peregrines, gyrfalcons, rough-legged hawks, and common ravens (functional raptors). On our trip we found one family of ravens and one

family of peregrines, both nesting on the abandoned structures at Lonely.

When humans build a tower, or a building, they open the
door to birds that eat other birds. One of the reasons geese
choose to enjoy their flightless days on the Teshekpuk (and
not the Colville) is precisely the low density of aerial predators.

Humans also attract and support predators with their
waste. Gulls, foxes, and bears are all drawn to landfills. This
unnatural resource increases their populations by increasing
their breeding success and survival rate (i.e., helping predators get through the lean times that are among nature's principal pruning mechanisms).

But these are just the front-end impacts that oil exploration and development would have on the Teshekpuk. It's the
long-term consequences of our species's dependence upon oil
that will, ultimately, prove more challenging to the Arctic and
its wildlife. We'd already seen some of those changes. We were
about to encounter more.

RELEASING THE GENIE
"Pah," I said, giving force to, and pronouncement upon, the
filtered water I'd just taken into my mouth. "This one's brackish, too."

"Looks better inland," Bob noted, nodding west. "Little
higher. We'll find drinkable water there, I'll bet."

It was a new experience for me. In my many trips into the
Arctic, I'd rarely had trouble finding potable water. In summer, across much of the Arctic, you are literally standing in it.
The mass of low-lying plants and peaty matter below is like a
supersaturated sponge. The underlying permafrost prevents

surface water from percolating away. The insulating mat of flowers, moss, and lichen retards evaporation.

Despite annual rainfall levels of fewer than ten inches a year, much of the coastal plain is semiaquatic. It's one of the reasons the Arctic enjoys a superabundance of mosquitoes during the warmer months. It's also the reason most oil exploration and extraction activity occurs during winter. The damage done to the fragile tundra surface is diminished when vehicles aren't churning up the surface and dormant plants are protected by a layer of snow.

The three of us were poised on the edge of a tundra polygon, a very common formation on sparsely vegetated tundra caused by perpetual freezing and thawing. Seen from the air, polygonal tundra looks like a patchwork quilt or a jigsaw puzzle composed of multisided geometric forms.

If you can remember back to the time when you made a cross section of an onion and looked at it under a microscope, take that microscopic image of straight-sided plant cells and superimpose it over the Arctic plain. In fact, the comparison of plant cells and polygon formations can go even further. The foot-high embankments that form the borders of the polygons are much like the structurally hard cell walls of plants. They hold ground water in the way cell walls surround and support the rich broth of life within.

What's fascinating about polygons is the extraordinary diversity in plants and animals they support—micro universes within the macro tundra.

The elevated banks support plants suited for a dry environment (despite their proximity to water). They serve as nesting places for tundra birds. Support runways for lemmings. Provide elevated perches for anything that wants a heads-up over the Arctic—jaegers searching for prey, breeding dunlin aspiring not to become prey.

Commonly, the centers of polygons hold standing water—shallow ponds brimming with newly emerged insect life. They host nesting phalaropes and provide avenues of retreat for young.

Between the dry, highland borders and aquatic interior there is, depending upon elevation and drainage, a measure of marsh and bog supporting another array of plants and animals.

Imagine. An entire Arctic environment housed in a formation the size of a two- or three-car garage. Multiply this by a few million polygonal building lots. Add a few big lakes and a wealth of smaller ones, a few well-drained higher areas, a meandering stream or two, and lots of open space, and you've got the Teshekpuk.

Or at least you had the Teshekpuk. What Bob, Linda, and I were discovering was the impact of an environmental shift that was, literally, changing the face of the tundra. An encroaching intrusion of salt water from the Beaufort Sea.

We were, now, almost two miles from camp, and the water in the lakes and polygonal pools was still brackish. The tidal inundation of this low and vulnerable coastline was an ecological game changer. It was the reason Bob had so much difficulty squaring what he could see from the air with the features on his topographic map. It was why the area around our camp was so vegetatively impoverished. Dry, dusty; largely devoid of living things.

The absence of buffering winter ice was leaving the shoreline unprotected from flooding and wave action. The impact of rising sea levels on all the world's low-lying coastal areas was threatening the low-lying Teshekpuk, too.

This dramatic habitat alteration has been linked to environmental changes associated with the back end of our species's oil addiction or, more explicitly, its exhaust.

It is unlikely that a person exists who has not been made aware of the global concern about climate change and the multiple impacts rising temperatures are going to have upon the planet. Anyone so apprised must also know that thermal-blanketing greenhouse gases in the atmosphere, resulting from the burning of fossil fuels, are widely held to be responsible for the rapid rise in temperature worldwide.

What you may not know is that the impact of global warming is most pronounced in the Arctic, where average temperatures have risen at a rate two times greater than the world average. The rate of change, as measured by the shrinkage of the Arctic icecap, already exceeds what was, just a few years ago, considered the worst-case scenario. Even if humans stopped adding to the earth's existing blanket of greenhouse gases, the warming process is, likely, already self-sustaining. The genie is out of the bottle. The Arctic, it turns out, is a great big carbon-dioxide-trapping bottle. We've already pulled the cork.

Let's return, for a moment, to that carbon chain. The one forged from plants by welding carbon atom to carbon atom using the energy of sunlight. Remember I said that the foundation of oil is organic matter that has settled in an anaerobic, or oxygen-deprived, place? Carbon atoms readily bond with oxygen atoms, and, given half a chance, they will. The process is called "oxidation" or "combustion." The result is most commonly a new compound called "carbon dioxide" and the release of the pent-up energy that was being stored.

Of course, all we were interested in was the energy. The carbon dioxide byproduct of combustion, which has been accumulating in the atmosphere, was pretty much ignored until it was implicated as one of the primary causal agents of climate change. The burning of fossil fuel is not, of course, the only source of carbon being emitted into the atmosphere. Heck, you add to the carbon footprint with every breath you exhale, every crackling blaze in your fireplace. Every forest or grass fire releases the magic that is energy and the evil genie that is carbon dioxide into the air.

Carbon is stored in many vaults within the earth, not just coal and oil (in fact, much of the earth's carbon is dissolved in the oceans), but one of those vaults, it turns out, is the permafrost that underlies the tundra. More than two thousand feet deep in places, this enduring cold-storage bin has been holding an estimated 14 percent of the world's carbon in cold suspension for about thirty thousand years. There is mounting evidence that the permafrost layer is already warming and melting, not just along the edges, as Linda, Bob, and I witnessed, but in the upper stratum of the interior—a stratum that underlies, and literally supports, most of the Arctic, including much of Alaska. This meltdown is not only releasing carbon dioxide into the atmosphere (accelerating global warming) but also releasing water into the world's oceans, which will add to rising sea levels.

The melting of the Arctic icecap, it turns out, will not influence ocean water levels. The volume contraction resulting from ocean ice being converted to water will balance the volume of water being added as the ice melts. However, the volume of water derived from terrestrial sources—melting glaciers on Greenland and melting permafrost—will very definitely contribute to rising sea levels.

At current estimates, sea levels are expected to rise twenty inches by the year 2100 (with upper estimates closer to thirty). By that time, most of the Teshekpuk will have eroded back into the sea, and future battles for oil, should our species still want the stuff, will be focused upon securing offshore drilling rights.

And the brant, who fly here every year for the security they require during their most vulnerable period? Good question.

BOIL OF GEESE

About four miles from camp (almost halfway back to Lonely), we decided to have lunch on a section of tundra still elevated above the reach of tides. It was wet, of course, but freshwater wet. We settled on one of the walls of a particularly well fortified polygon (which had also won the favor of a pair of pomarine jaegers) and broke into our packs—exhuming all the standard edibles of a Wilderness Birding Adventures picnic.

The jaegers, pirate princes of the coastal plain, watched our every move—for both threat and opportunity. We didn't pose much of a threat. Clearly the large, black-capped, charcoal brown birds had a nest nearby, and, being responsible, we didn't want to stress them.

But we did present an opportunity. The Teshekpuk region, that year, was rich in lemmings; as rich as Bylot Island was not. Every one of these tailless rodents that our antics sent scampering was one less that a jaeger had to find on its own (and we dislodged many).

"Gotcha," Bob announced, throwing his Wilderness Birding Adventures cap (and half of his six-foot, three-inch frame) flat across the tundra.

"Missed 'im," Linda corrected, betting on the survival-honed quickness of lemmings and the age-dampened reflexes of Bob. "Pass the peanut butter, please."

"What were you going to do if you caught him?" I asked, helping myself to a wedge of smoked salmon to accompany the cream-cheese-laden bagel in my hand.

"Add him to tonight's chili," Bob rejoindered, after recovering his poise (if not his pride). Returning his lemmingless hat to his head. Reaching for and offering the requested peanut butter. Pausing long enough to remove a smoked sausage from the pack and reduce it to bite-size pieces with his belt knife.

It was just about this time that we heard the hum of a distant aircraft and found it, too. A single-engine Piper Cub, flying low and slow over the eastern horizon, surveying the territory east of Pogik Bay.

"Must be the Fish and Wildlife survey team doing their waterfowl count," Bob assessed, and this seemed to be so. For half an hour, we watched the plane patrol in ever-closing sweeps—an aerial harrier, flying a search pattern over waterfowl-bearing lakes. It wasn't close enough to be intrusive. Three miles at least, probably more.

That's why the boil of geese, charging over the horizon and heading straight for us, seemed at first unrelated to the plane. But it was clear that the birds were fleeing from something, and as the mass drew closer, and nothing else appeared, we were led to conclude that the flightless birds were, indeed, reacting to the survey plane.

A single plane, flying a search pattern that would not even intercept the geese, was enough to prompt the birds to retreat, at a dead run. I don't know how far they had run before we spotted them. But they crossed at least a mile while we watched, never slackening their pace. It seemed like they were set to run right over us, a prospect that did not sit well with the jaeger.

When the geese were about two hundred yards out, the jaeger took wing, flew directly at the mass of birds, and, singling out one member of the flock, pinned it to the ground and proceeded to rip feathers from its neck.

A greater white-fronted goose is a sizable bird—at four and a half pounds, almost four times the weight of the jaeger. But the goose was completely mastered, and after ten punishing seconds the jaeger lifted off, returning to his perch. The geese, recovering from the attack, regrouped and resumed their original course.

Realizing that the geese seemed not to have gotten the message, once more the jaeger took wing. Selected another member of the flock. Subjected this individual to the same foot-pummeling, feather-ripping punishment doled out to the first bird.

This time, the geese seemed to get it. They altered course, veering north, passing wide of us. The jaeger returned to his sentinel perch as if nothing unusual had happened.

The geese were still heading for the horizon when we packed up lunch and continued on. I have no way of knowing whether the birds did or did not figure in this year's census, but one thing I can tell you: everything Ted said about the hypersensitivity of molting geese appeared to be not only true but understated.

We spent four nights at Bunny. The weather remained fair but windy. Windy enough for me to conclude that the reason mosquitoes were not more in evidence was that, if they tried to launch themselves, they'd get their wings blown off. Windy enough that the fine, organic dust left in the wake of the tidally blown-out coast became an integral part of our diet, sleeping quarters, and the air we breathed. When the fog rolled in, it turned to aerosol goo.

With the wind to our backs, the return trip to Lonely took less than a day—which was fortunate. The morning after our return, the wind shifted back to the north and the pack ice snugged back up against the coast. Had we lingered at Bunny, we would have been there awhile, trapped between ice and a blown-out coast.

TIDE OF BATTLE

Breathing hard, I used my newly heightened archaeological interest as an excuse to catch my breath.

"Two-mile walk, my foot," I said, looking back toward the Lonely DEW line station, shimmering to the east. "I hope the guy counts geese better than he estimates distance."

The guy, by the way, was a young waterfowl biologist working for the U.S. Geological Survey, named Keith, whom we found bivouacked at Lonely upon our return. He and another biologist were engaged in a six-week effort to get a handle on the number of geese using the Teshekpuk region. It was their survey plane we'd seen.

Over a generously offered, and gratefully accepted, mug of fresh-pressed coffee, he asked whether I'd "hiked over to the ruins down the beach yet." An old "whaling station," he speculated.

"About how far?" I asked.

"Two miles," he said, casually.

I accepted this estimate at face value. Putting more stock in his earnest brown eyes than in his wiry frame. "Two miles" to a field-fit, thirty-year-old biologist translates to four miles to an out-of-shape, fifty-six-year-old bird observatory director (and to the measurement standards accepted by the rest of the world, too, I might add). Still, it's hard to think ill of someone who hands you a mug of semiexcellent French roast coffee five hundred miles from the nearest espresso bar (and the truth is, I would have visited the ruins anyway).

Keith's lair was one of the outlying sheds that served the Lonely complex. Several more decommissioned buildings were being used by the Husky Oil Company. Their posted signs were much in evidence, and, curiously enough, those same signs, bearing the Husky Oil, NPR Operations, Inc. brand were posted around the hilltop ruins in front of me along with the admonishment DO NOT DISTURB. ARCHEO-LOGICAL SITE. Husky Oil's jurisdiction within the National Petroleum Reserve was, evidently, broad based.

"Do not disturb" is not in semantic essence the same as "No trespassing," so I finished my climb. Set my back against a crumbling structure to enjoy the solitude and the view. The structure, an old sod-walled outhouse, had been recently appropriated by a nesting pair of snowy owls if the surfeit of pellets lying about was any clue.

The view of the ice-choked Beaufort Sea, the mud flats to the west, and the pond-pocked tundra to the south was magnificent. Lonely, almost dead east, rippled like an illusion. The owls sure knew how to pick their lookout points.

I wondered how many thousands of Native hunters had stood on this same hilltop for the same reason. I wondered about structures on the site. Six (or so) slat-sided and sod-reinforced buildings, only one that deserved to be called "standing." Several paces north were two wooden dories whose derelict keels were welded to the tundra by moss and lichen. An owl pellet's toss to the south, a frost-shattered mound sprouted splintered coffins and human remains.

I learned later, from a 1982 report filed by Edwin S. Hall Jr. of the U.S. Geological Survey, that the graves had been inadvertently exposed by Husky Oil crews in the late 1970s. The report identified the site, and buildings, as a former trapping and trading center and noted its location as about "one hundred yards from the coast."

At the time of my visit, the coast was less than fifty feet away. Half of the smaller of the two dories, identified in the report as "whaleboats," projected over the edge of the eroded cliff. Another part of Alaska's cultural heritage, it seemed, was about to wash away.

Chewee?

I looked up to see one of the millions of snow buntings that enliven the Arctic landscape looking down on me. The bird seemed puzzled, but not troubled, by my intrusion. Like the many snow buntings that had made themselves at home in the ruins of Lonely, this bird was taking advantage of the habitat-altering opportunities left by members of our species.

Snow buntings are cavity nesters. They fit their feather-lined nests in whatever protective nooks and crannies they can find, so the abandoned radar site offered a surfeit of prime man-made nest sites. Every warping board, every pile of crates bought and paid for by taxpayer money or oil-company profits constitutes prime nesting real estate for snow buntings.

Of course I explored Lonely. What child of the Cold War could resist the temptation to see, firsthand, one of the celebrated outposts that protected us from communism?

As anyone growing up in the post–World War II era knows, the surrender of Germany and Japan did not usher in an era of peace. Instead, the conflict shifted and went underground as the war's two most powerful victors, the United States and the Soviet Union, squared off in a protracted game of ideological and political chicken. The stakes were high. Both sides had nuclear weapons and delivery systems capable of annihilating their adversaries (not to mention life on Earth). What's more, the political and economic systems of both nations quickly became enmeshed in and nurtured by the conflict. Or don't you remember President Dwight David Eisenhower's "military-industrial complex" speech?

Neither side trusted the other. Both believed that survival depended upon nuclear supremacy as a deterrent to attack. While the Cold War was fought on many fronts, the Arctic became the coldest and most remote battleground for this war of nerves and economic attrition.

In 1954 the American and Canadian governments decided to build a series of radar stations across their remote northern reaches, following roughly along the sixty-ninth parallel (two hundred miles north of the Arctic Circle), stretching from northern Alaska to Baffin Island, and later southern Greenland. Intended to offer early detection of a transpolar, manned bomber attack, the Distant Early Warning line had its usefulness compromised even before its completion by advances in Soviet missile technology. A number of the smaller DEW line radar stations were deactivated. By 1964, only the main stations remained operational.

One of these was the Lonely auxiliary radar station, officially designated POW-1. Located approximately one hundred miles east-southeast of Point Barrow, isolated by the Beaufort Sea on the north and low, flat, spongy tundra on the south, you could hardly find a more "lonely" outpost to fight a cold war than Lonely.

The station was finally deactivated in 1989. That is when the final battle of the Cold War began.

Cleanup. Owing to decades of supersaturation with fuel and PCBs, Lonely and not a few other relics of the Cold War are designated Superfund sites today.

It has always been one of our species's saddest legacies in the North. Since the early whaling days, no matter what type of equipment we cart into the Arctic, a portion, reduced to refuse, has always been left behind. It costs money to get stuff above the Arctic Circle. Few budgets, including military budgets, ever include the cost of getting broken or obsolete equipment out.

It's not for nothing that the fifty-five-gallon fuel drum has been called the "state flower of Alaska." Their rusting remains dot the tundra.

I first learned about the DEW line when I was in grade school. The radar sites were featured, as I recall, in a publication we were given called *Weekly Reader*. Another time there was an article about the world's first nuclear submarine, the *USS Nautilus*. It was the first submarine to cruise under the Arctic Icecap, which seemed perfectly normal since the United States was always first in everything.

Well, almost everything. Sputnik was a big surprise.

USS stood for United States ship. The *Nautilus* was a navy ship, and, just like the DEW line, it was something that was protecting us from the Soviet Union. I don't know whether anyone ever told me that the people who lived way over on the far side of the Arctic were evil. But since it was certain that the United States was the best country in the world, any country that didn't like us had to be bad, right?

At least the leaders were bad. The people were just "brainwashed."

Interestingly enough, the animals of the Arctic didn't seem able to distinguish between our side and their side, so they didn't take sides. The Arctic environment is circumpolar. The snow buntings you find in Alaska are the same snow buntings you find in Siberia. In fact, some birds, most notably water-fowl, ignored Cold War boundaries entirely. Some of the black brant and snow geese that molt around Teshekpuk actually nest in Siberia.

Despite the DEW line, and the *Nautilus,* and the fact that the United States was the most powerful nation on Earth, we were still taught, at school, what to do just in case the Soviet Union did try to bomb us. The exercise was called a "bomb drill." The difference between a "bomb drill" and a "fire drill" was that fire drills were sort of serious but bomb drills were *way* serious.

When the bell rang, we'd all push back from our desks (leaving the paper and crayons and *Weekly Readers* and everything else) and march, single file, into the hall, where we were instructed to sit, with our backs against the wall, hands folded over our heads and heads between our knees, then wait for the bell to ring. We weren't allowed to talk or laugh, and the teachers were serious and stern. I concluded that what we were doing was learning to behave like school kids in the Soviet Union. If we were afraid of them, then they must know something we didn't, like a secret judo hold or something.

We sat scrunched up for a terribly long time. Until our necks hurt and our butts went numb. I figured that what we were doing was a kind of training. When the war finally came, maybe the kids who kept their heads between their knees the longest would determine the outcome. I didn't want to be responsible for America losing a war, since America always won its wars, so I trained real hard and didn't complain.

We'll never know whether my determination would have turned the tide. We never had a war. Almost. Not quite. Then, nearly fifty years after the end of World War II, the Soviet Union stopped being our enemy. They even started calling themselves the Russians again, like they did before they became evil, and everything was fine.

With the threat of nuclear attack diminished, the DEW line sites were abandoned. They became homes for duck biologists, oil geologists, and snow buntings, and this détente was not limited to Alaska, Greenland, and Canada. The Soviet Union abandoned their northern military outposts, too.

In 1997, I was able to visit one of the Soviet Cold War enclaves, a submarine base tucked into the blown-out side of an old volcano that opened to the Bering Sea. It was a large base. Much bigger than a DEW line site. Linda and I and all the passengers aboard our ship were welcome to roam at will the buildings built by the Soviet state (unlike the buildings at Lonely, which have No Trespassing and Government Property signs posted all over them).

I don't know when the sub base was deactivated except after the end of the Cold War. Only one thing seems certain. It was abandoned very quickly. I say this because one of the buildings I entered was the school, where those other children of the Cold War were being trained. And on the desks were the crayons and papers and booklets they left behind. It was as though the bell had rung for a bomb drill. The children had filed out of the room. And never returned.

Sitting with my back against the outhouse, looking back at Lonely, I couldn't help but wonder how long these abandoned outposts, theirs and ours, would stand, how long the Arctic would suffer their presence. Sitting about a half mile from the coast, Lonely wasn't in any immediate danger of being erased by tide—unlike the old whaling station, which seemed destined to disappear in a year or two.

Even though these old Cold War enclaves represent history, I wonder whether it's a history anyone cares to remember. A cold war, fought on many fronts, but most graphically perhaps metaphorically, here in the Arctic—where the scars from a war that was waged but never fought mar the landscape today.

Who won? I guess the snow buntings and the ravens and the peregrine falcons. They got the buildings.

Unless, of course, the Soviet kids who left their crayons and papers and booklets on the desks at that sub base are all still sitting somewhere with their hands over their heads and their heads between their knees, waiting for the bell.

If this is so, then my hat's off to them. Those Soviet kids are way tougher than this American kid could ever hope to be.

CHAPTER 4

Moon Month of Saggaruut (July–August),
"Caribou Hair Sheds"

The Barren Lands

Northwest Territories, Canada

"There's a wolf down in the trees," Terry announced. In the scope of human utterances, there are few so galvanizing. In fact, after considerable thought, I came up with only three:

"Stop or I'll shoot."

"I'm pregnant."

"We got a letter from the IRS today."

But further reflection brought further refinement to even this very short list. The thought of a convocation with the IRS might be cause for apprehension (if you have something to hide), but it doesn't bring you to the balls of your feet. The directive "stop or I'll shoot" carries the implicit promise that compliance means safety.

As for "I'm pregnant," well, this is one that can cut two ways.

But "there's a wolf" is in a class to itself, and it affects your entire system. It makes hairs on the backs of necks tingle, hearts miss a beat, and stomach muscles tighten. It picks the lock on some deep, dark corner of our minds and brings every sense we know (and maybe some we don't) to hyperawareness.

There is only one response to "there's a wolf down in the trees," and every member of the group made it.

"Where? Where? Where? Where?" Nine *where*'s in all. Including mine. In the Canadian Arctic, awareness is nine tenths of survival, and you need not live here to understand this. This brand of wisdom is carried in the blood.

"Okay," our guide said, "if you look across the open flat, you'll see three mounds, okay? Go to the rightmost mound, okay? Go slightly right and back to the trees and . . ."

It took two minutes before all members of the group located the animal, standing about six hundred yards away. The reaction time might have been shortened if Terry spoke French. Five members of the group were from France and had traveled to northern Canada expressly to see wolves. It might also have helped if Terry had thought to add that the animal was white. Even at six hundred yards and without binoculars, a white wolf, standing in front of a dark green wall of stunted spruce trees, is hard to miss.

"I should have brought the spotting scope," I lamented to Linda, who was still waiting for Terry to return her binoculars.

"I should have brought a camera with a big lens," she returned.

"It never occurred to me that we'd run into something like this on a short walk after dinner."

"Especially since the outgoing group said they hadn't seen a wolf, right?"

"Right. Just a couple of pups at a den. No adults."

"This is fantastic."

"Unbelievable."

"Magnifique!"

And then the animal was gone.

It didn't leap. It didn't run. It simply walked into the trees with an easy, long-limbed stride. Everything about it cried "wolf."

The spontaneous eruption of joy and congratulations would have gone on longer except for Linda's observation. "It's back."

And so it was. Back at the edge of the trees. A curtain call from an animal that has, for human ages, shunned both the spotlight and the stage.

It started to move again. A lupine vapor that materialized and dematerialized as it made its way through the trees to emerge on the far side of the lake, where it paused and urinated behind a bush to mark its territory. It seemed, for all the world, as if this animal wanted to be seen.

"Did it squat?" Terry wanted to know.

"It did," I said.

"The female then," he noted.

"Seems like," I agreed, and probability sided with this assessment. The esker we were on was a traditional den site, and females commonly stay with the pups while the males hunt. Wolf pups, numbering four to five, are born in April, so chances were, in mid-July, they were still in the vicinity, probably still in the den.

An esker, by the way, is a pile of glacial scat. The sandy refuse, forged in the bowels of glaciers, that settles to earth when the glacier melts. This one was about the size of an industrial park. The Barren Lands are overrun with them.

The adult animal continued along the lakeshore, quartering to our left, circling us. She didn't hurry. She seemed, in fact, almost indifferent—which could hardly have been the case.

We were intruders in *her* territory. Mother wolves with young are hardly indifferent to that.

The animal went into a ravine, then appeared again a scant 250 yards away, sat, and turned appraising eyes upon us. We couldn't believe our fortune.

This was not the first time Linda and I have knowingly been studied by wolves. But there are times when I'd like to forget that misadventure. We didn't exactly do our species proud that day.

Splashes with Wolves

It was on the fourth day of our raft trip down the Kongakut— two days after the Fourth of July parade. Two rafts, both filled with people and gear. It was midmorning, and we'd just gotten under way when Diane, the artist, announced: "I saw two animals disappear into the thicket up ahead."

Odd, I thought, that she wasn't more specific. We'd been seeing caribou off and on for two days. Caribou would have been the likely animal. But for some reason, Diane had chosen to be vague. And why had the animals gone into the thicket? Caribou were crossing the river, not paralleling it.

Muskoxen were certainly a possibility. These shaggy, Pleistocene relics are partial to riverside thickets and fairly common in the Arctic National Wildlife Refuge. Moose, too. Still . . .

My unspoken hope was that the animals would turn out to be grizzly bears—so, very probably, a female and her half-grown cub. Male bears are loners.

There was little time for speculation. The river was moving swiftly. In less than a minute both rafts were abreast the thicket—our raft in the middle of the river, the other hugging the steep bank.

"There they are," Linda announced. "Oh my god, they're wolves!"

And so they were. A black one and a gray one. Standing slightly back of the riverbank. Fifteen feet above us, a mere fifty feet away. Calmly taking our measure. The other raft was so close to the bank they couldn't see the animals standing above them. In a frenzy of uncoordinated paddle strokes, the four occupants propelled their raft to the far side of the river, which would have been a fine strategy if the river hadn't been moving so fast and if there had been any place to land.

The show of human incompetence that ensued might represent the very lowest point in the relationship between humans and wolves (as viewed from the human perspective). As the raft bounced against the bank, one of its occupants was dislodged from his seat on the downstream side and into what must have been, as indicated by the expression on his face, very cold water. His cross-bow companion jumped into the water to try to stabilize the boat, only to lose his footing and be dragged into the water by the force of the current.

With two members of our party now in the river, our raft

hastened to the rescue and further aggravated the situation by broadsiding the other raft, knocking the river's first victim, who had just stood up, back into the current.

The wolves, still poised on the far bank, calmly watched the whole Keystone Kops routine. One was so captivated that he eased back on his haunches. The other transformed his mouth into a wolfish grin, and if telecommunication is something wolves practice, then their unspoken conversation must have gone something like this:

"Have you ever seen such incompetence in your life?"

"If caribou were this inept, the tundra would be paved with steaks."

"Do you have any idea why we're supposed to be circumspect around these bozos?"

"Haven't a clue. But the grayling along that riverbank are sure taking a beating."

"Yeah, it would suck to be a grayling right about now. Ever tasted grayling?"

"No. You?"

"Yeah. Pretty good. Good as char. Oh! I think the big guy's setting up for another dunking."

"Caribou loin says you're wrong."

"You're on."

After our party had gained a measure of control, and while our sodden and shivering companions began shedding their clothes, the standing wolf lifted his leg, directing a squirt of harsh judgment onto a rock, and trotted off. His seated companion, with seeming reluctance, rose and joined him.

But that was then. Happily, on this occasion, we humans were comporting ourselves with more dignity. Or so we thought.

So what is it about wolves that is so galvanizing and polarizing? Their history and ours, their steps and ours, have walked the same paths for a very long time. They figure in our tales and legends. Their name and attributes have crept into our vocabulary. They are lightning rods when it comes to present-day debates concerning wilderness and land use.

Yes, they are powerful animals. The jaws of a wolf are strong enough to crack the leg bones of caribou and muskox to get at the marrow within. Yes, they are predatory. Unlike grizzly bears, who augment their diets with roots and berries, wolves eat nothing but meat. Adult males may tip the scales at two hundred pounds (females are smaller). They hunt singly and in pairs but most effectively in packs (and it is not for nothing that German U-boats, in World War II, adopted the name and tactics of a "wolf pack"). They use coordinated intelligence to bring down animals the size of moose, and, yes, there are even authenticated cases of people being killed by healthy, wild wolves.

In North America, there is precisely one. A twenty-two-year-old engineering student who was killed in northern Saskatchewan in 2005. There are other documented attacks and fatalities in Europe and Asia. But even among people who live in proximity to wolves, the chance of being attacked (much less fatally injured) is considerably less than that of being killed by domestic animals—including dogs, who are descended from wolves. Interestingly enough, the fatal attack upon the young geologist occurred in an area where wolves were frequenting a garbage dump and had thus become habituated to people. Perhaps familiarity breeds contempt with wolves, too.

But why would our species let the domesticated kin of wolves in the front door and barricade the back? I don't know—unless it is for the same reasons our species is both fascinated by and fearful of wolves.

At most times, and in most cultures, wolves have been worshiped and admired for their prowess, intelligence, and pack mentality. The orphaned twins and future founders of Rome, Romulus and Remus, were, according to legend, rescued and raised by a female wolf, and the Roman Empire has seen no equal in history. The legends of Native American peoples frequently involve wolves and accord praise to their cunning and courage (among the Pawnee, the sign language symbols for the people and the wolf are nearly identical).

It was only when humans turned from hunting to herding that wolves began to fall out of favor. The Old and the New Testaments are replete with references to the rapaciousness and guileful nature of wolves. That's the same Old Testament that tells the story of Abel, whose offering of lamb was accepted by God (while his brother, Cain's garden produce was not) and the same New Testament that makes frequent metaphoric references like "the flock," the "lamb of God," and "the Good Shepherd."

The ancient Hebrews were very definitely shepherds, and, as such, they didn't have a lot of good feelings for wolves. When Christianity was transported (by Roman roads) to what would someday become Europe, missionaries found a mixed bag of lupine lore already in place. German culture was generally partial to wolves. Scandinavians, on the other hand, saw wolves as sinister. This witches' brew of ancient lore and Christian antipathy probably spawned the werewolf myth that prevailed in medieval Europe and raged through France in the

1600s, resulting in the execution of hundreds of innocent humans (or half humans, depending on your convictions).

In the end, it wasn't myth or even religion that proved the downfall of wolves in Europe and later across most of North America. It was persecution by landowners who adopted a strike-first policy with regard to animals that might threaten their livestock coupled with the destruction of the large forested tracts that are, over much of its range, the wolf's stronghold. In more modern times, a faction of sports hunters, state game councils, and some biologists, too, has sought to reduce wolf numbers in order to increase populations of game animals, such as caribou and moose. In 2007, a bounty on wolves was reinstituted by Alaska Fish and Game over the howled protests of environmentalists.

Wolves were extirpated from England in the 1500s and from Scotland in the 1700s. Today, in reduced numbers, they are found in Spain, Scandinavia, Germany, Italy, Eastern Europe, Russia, Israel, and much of Asia. In North America, where wolves once ranged from the High Arctic to northern Mexico, the animal is now found in perhaps a dozen northern states (where it is something of a tourist attraction). Most wolf aspirants head farther north, to Canada and Alaska, where the majority of North America's estimated sixty to seventy thousand wolves reside. Despite these numbers, the chances of actually seeing the animals are slim.

Years of persecution have made them shy. Wolves' skills as predators have made them stealthy. Over much of their range they are most active at night. All of these qualities make wolves hard to see in the wild. This explains the jubilation of our group at the sight of an adult animal a mere 250 yards away.

· · ·

Eyes

If our initial contact with the ivory-colored wolf was unbridled excitement, this closer encounter was jubilation bordering on awe. When the wolf's curiosity seemed finally satisfied, she rose, stretched, and, turning back toward the den, disappeared once again into the trees.

At first, we were speechless. Then everyone was speaking at once. Linda, Bruce, and his father, Gail, who were bemoaning the absence of their cameras. Jacques and Sophie and Roman, his wife and son, were probably doing the same thing (just in French). Our guide, Terry, was trying to impart a measure of interpretive lore.

It was a magic moment. Our very first night in Canada's famed Barren Lands, and we'd already seen a wolf. For many in our group, it was the fulfillment of a lifelong ambition.

I don't know how long we dawdled. Five minutes, maybe ten. Our watches showed 10:15. The sun was poised just above the horizon, and dusk was settling in. Time for all diurnal creatures to head for the safety of their dens.

We turned to go home and . . .

The wolf was standing behind us. She'd feinted right, then, hidden by the trees, headed left. She had circled us to get the wind in her favor and was now between us and camp. She was close enough that through binoculars you could see the amber surrounding the small, dark portals of her eyes. She was, by her presence and her stance, saying, "I win."

That is when the hair on the back of my neck began to tingle, my heart skipped a beat, my stomach squirmed, and dark, unnamable fears started to squirm about in my mind. "I win" translates to "you lose." And standing on that sandy esker, with night now poised to eclipse the day, I felt in my blood what millions of animals over thousands of years must have cried in their minds in their last moments of life.

I have been outmatched by a wolf.

Minutes passed. We knew we had to break the stalemate by moving forward. Unless we did, we'd be walking home in the dark.

The wolf did nothing for a time, merely watched our approach. Then once again she turned and disappeared. We hurried to the spot. Knelt to examine the single set of tracks leading straight away. Followed them with our eyes to the point where they entered into the trees and . . .

Maybe the others believed that there was nothing there. That the wolf had finished toying with us. That her sole objective had been to lure us away from the den.

I knew better, knew it in my blood. Twice now I'd been fooled by this wolf. My wits told me what my blood confirmed, and that was that, somewhere behind those shadows, there were eyes.

"What are you staring at?" Linda wanted to know.

"Nothing," I said, which was honest enough. "Shadows."

"Well, that was pretty amazing," she said. And it was. Memorable and amazing. The high point of the trip to the Barren Lands of northwest Canada for an anticipated rendezvous with caribou.

It was all downhill from here.

SIX MONTHS EARLIER; MAURICETOWN, NEW JERSEY
"Who?" I said to Linda, who was recently returned from the NANPA (North American Nature Photography Association) convention and had a fistful of promotional literature to prove it.

"Goes by the name Esker Al," she said. "Not his real name, I'm sure," she added, and I affirm that this is true. Fact is, Linda produced a different moniker altogether. Esker Al is the name I just invented for the sake of this recounting.

"And the name of the company?" I invited.

"Superior Barren Lands Ecotours," she didn't say because, like the surrogate name of the proprietor, this isn't the real name of the company.

Why am I being so circumspect?

Because, having now recovered from our disappointing week with EA, I find myself oddly sympathetic to his plight; less interested in venting than in treating readers to a good story and an important lesson.

We were, at the time of our conversation, deep in the planning stages of this book. We were sure we knew the elements we wanted to include. The challenge, as it has always been in the Arctic, was logistics.

Going to the Arctic is not like going to Yellowstone National Park, or the Everglades, or any number of other ecotourist destinations. Even now, in the twenty-first century, there are precious few all-season roads that intrude into this northern wilderness. Early explorers paddled or walked. In the winter, after the snow falls and rivers freeze, seasonal "ice roads" open to truck traffic.

After World War I, airplanes made the region more accessible, but at a price—both human and material. Bush pilots are a select breed. Those who survive to retirement have storehouses of stories to tell. Those who don't survive, who end up "augering in" to the side of a cloud-shrouded cliff or losing power and ditching in the trees, add poignancy to those stories.

Little has changed since airpower was introduced to the

Arctic—except for the volume of air traffic. Year by year the search for mineral riches accelerates and the desire for wilderness experiences among fishermen, hunters, canoeists, and nature enthusiasts increases. But forays onto the tundra still require planning, coordination, and logistical support.

You can do it on your own, and some people do. Or you can hook up with guides or enterprises that offer an infrastructure already in place so that you can spend more time enjoying and less time organizing and improvising.

You don't have to build the railroad. All you have to do is run your train down someone else's track. The trick is finding a railroad that works and connects to places you want to go. The train Linda and I wanted to take was the Caribou Express, and it led to one of the planet's most celebrated natural events: the post-breeding migrations of caribou.

Every year, just when spring begins to swirl as a rumor at the edge of the great northern forests, several distinct and geographically disjunct caribou herds start their annual trek from southern wintering areas, close to tree line, to historic calving grounds, on the open tundra. Pushing through wind-deepened snow, crossing mountain passes, the animals arrive just in time to drop their calves in what amounts to one big communal birthing before turning around and taking a long and meandering route back to the shelter of the trees—their several-day-old calves in tow.

It is an amazing sight, involving tens of thousands of lichen-munching, hoof-clicking ungulates. It would be unthinkable to write a book on the Arctic and not include the migration of caribou.

But where? And how? There might be millions of caribou, but there were also many millions of acres of tundra.

The breeding and wintering grounds are prescribed, but the routes are not. They vary year to year depending upon ground and weather conditions and, to a great degree and unlikely as it may sound, wind direction.

By the time caribou drop their calves, the most ferocious predators in the north lands are on the prowl. No, not wolves. Mosquitoes. The bloodsucking hordes descend upon caribou like, well, like bloodsucking hordes. Relief comes in numbers. Keep together, let the animals around you guard your flanks and siphon off their share of the misery.

The other way caribou keep their heads while among the bugs is to keep their heads ahead of the bugs—i.e., by walking into the wind. Fighting a headwind forces the mosquitoes to work harder to keep up with the herd, and it probably reduces the overall number of mosquitoes that are going to home in on a blood meal.

Mosquitoes are able to detect and target carbon dioxide—a mammal's primary exhaust. When caribou keep the wind in their faces, the only mosquitoes that are going to be aware of the animals' passage are the ones the caribou are going to kick up anyway.

So caribou move in accordance with the wind, and wind direction on the tundra, several months out, is no more predictable than it is anywhere else. In order to intercept the migration, you need to be flexible, you need to be mobile, and you need good, reliable, up-to-the-minute intelligence.

EA's literature seemed to offer all these things: "aircraft reconnaissance, GPS positioning, and satellite communications combined with nearly four decades of traditional guiding knowledge." As the write-up on the trips that fit our time slot allowed: "The aircraft is an integral part to the success of the caribou portion of the trips. Ongoing aerial reconnaissance & field communications are conducted to watch for the caribou herd. . . . Toward the end of the week and once the caribou herd is located . . . we will then attempt to move participants to a vantage point from which they can view and photograph this incredible phenomenon." The literature explained that this attempt might necessitate relocation to a "spike camp"—an impromptu camp away from the main camp, but that was okay with us.

"What do you think?"

"I dunno. What do you think?"

"I think I'd like to talk to a few people who have been to the camp."

"Well," Linda said. "Galen Rowell's picture is on the website."

"Galen Rowell's dead," I reminded her.

"I know that," she said. "I'm not saying we should do it. I'm just saying that we should look into it."

And we did. Called EA—a husky-voiced Canadian who spoke with barroom volume and a salesman's glibness. Discussed our objectives and our plans. Agreed with him that the second caribou trip in July 2007 offered greater potential for success. Declined his recommendation to add another week in order to maximize our opportunities. We hemmed. Hawed. Considered less costly options. But in the end we bought our tickets, to the territorial capital of Yellowknife, then on to the Native hamlet of K., and took our chances.

THE MAKINGS OF A DISAPPOINTMENT

The northern frontier is, and has always been, poisonous to plans. Nothing there ever seems to go according to schedule. Everything happens at the last minute. Things such as pumps, generators, and aircraft break with a regularity that borders on routine. Bush pilots keep schedules that are only tangent with the rest of us.

Those who travel in the Arctic cover their bases with good organization and planning, built-in time buffers, two of everything that cannot be reconstructed on the spot, and, most of all, outfitters they can depend upon.

Then they cross their fingers and bring lots of reading material.

There were little, and largely unheeded, signs that our trip in search of caribou was not going to be without challenges. After we'd sent our money, communications from EA pretty nearly dried up. Linda's efforts to secure lodging in K. at the establishment recommended in the company's literature met with repeated failure. Something, we learned later, to do with a "plumbing" problem.

The native hamlet of K., a town occupied principally by members of the Dene Nation, or First People, was not designed with tourism in mind, or, as the manager of the village co-op put it, "there is no tourist infrastructure here."

We were instructed, finally, to call Brenda's Bed and Breakfast, which Linda did. And while she thought it was odd that the person she spoke to didn't care to register our names, Linda took the operational nonchalance in stride. Things are pretty casual in the North.

One possible explanation for this nonchalance surfaced the day we arrived—along with six other EA patrons whose reservations were also anonymous (synonymous with nonexistent). Brenda was out of town. Her daughter, who knew less about our lodging arrangements than we did, threw a fit.

In the end, as things tend to, everything worked out. The six other patrons, who were supposed to go on a canoe trip brokered by EA, flew out on an impromptu flight that night. Halfway through their preparation of dinner, a bush plane arrived with their name on it. They hastily assembled their gear, invited us to "enjoy the meal," and left.

Linda and I fell in with a father and son from California, forty-five-year-old Bruce, a professor at U.C. Santa Barbara, and his seventy-five-year-old father, Gail, a retired DuPont employee.

They were on our tour and were in it primarily for the promise of wolves. They had arrived the previous day. Discovered, as we had, that there was no means of transportation for people or gear from the landing strip to the B & B—a distance of two miles. The van promised by EA was "broken."

This is probably as good a place as any to stop referring to Brenda's B & B by that title. The truth is, one of those *B*s is superfluous (unless it stands for "bathroom"), because, while the rate of $139 U.S. per person, per night did cover a bed, it didn't cover breakfast (except that which you prepared yourself). That said, the place was tidy and adequately equipped. The shower water was hot. The coffeemaker worked. The residents of K. were cordial and indulgent.

Word came to us, via the co-op manager, that a plane would pick us up the next day between 1:00 and 4:00.

"No matter what happens, we should all stick together," Bruce both counseled and pleaded. We agreed, and we did. Bruce and Gail proved to be delightful companions and experienced off-road travelers.

We got to the airstrip the next day, dislodging, from his

bed atop a baggage cart, a tall, gaunt, intense-looking man of forty-five who identified himself as Terry and announced that he was going to be our guide for the week. Even at the beginning of the trip, he looked much like the rugged, trail-worn people you find pictured in the Patagonia catalog at the ends of their trips.

Armed with years of guiding experience, cursed with a bad back resulting from an old "rock and roll" injury, Terry allowed that he had stopped working for EA four years earlier and hadn't been to the camp since. He had been entreated to return two weeks before. Had declined. Been contacted again two days prior. This time, for undisclosed reasons, he'd accepted. He caught a hastily arranged flight to Yellowknife. Got to K. not knowing when a bush plane might be meeting him.

He'd missed a meal or two and gratefully accepted a granola bar. He informed us that the five other members of our group were already waiting in the small building that served as the K. airport. A couple and a father-mother-son trio—all from France, all enticed to the Arctic by the promise of wolves.

Seemed Linda and I were the only ones in it for the caribou.

About four o'clock, a single-engine de Havilland Otter touched down. Disgorged four passengers. Whisked Terry and the French contingent off to Esker Al's camp, promising to return for the four of us in about two and a half hours.

Bruce, Gail, Linda, and I went back to the airport waiting room, which we shared with the plane's offloaded passengers—two men and a woman and her daughter. One of the men, a tall, thin, bearded gentleman from New South Wales, seemed tensely out of sorts. The other fellow, a more compact and contemplative man in his late thirties (who worked

as an animator for a celebrated screenwriter), seemed tired—
and with good reason. For close to a week, he'd been skipping
sleep in the hope of seeing a wolf.

The mother-daughter combination looked like they'd survived the Inquisition—barely. All, it turned out, were returning veterans of EA's first wolf and caribou camp of the season.

VETERANS' SAY

"Soooo . . . how was it?" I invited, curious to see who might
rise to the invitation.

"Interesting," the taller, bearded man said, managing,
somehow, to pronounce all four syllables through unmoving
lips and clenched teeth.

"Are you going out there?" the animator asked.

"Hope to," I said, smiling.

"Good luck," he said.

"Bad?" I asked.

"A little organization might have helped," the bearded gentleman assessed. This time he moved his lips.

The mother-daughter duo remained silent, but Daughter,
who looked to be about twelve, put her head in Mom's lap,
seeking and finding emotional support but no escape from
the misery she must have been experiencing. When they'd
first stepped off the plane, I'd thought they were burn victims.
Their exposed skin, looking pink and raw, seemed to be coming off in chunks. Only in the confines of the airport lounge
did I realize that what looked like flash burns from a nuclear
blast was, in reality, lavishly applied calamine lotion.

If EA's camp offered nothing else, it sure looked like it had
a wealth of biting insects.

Over the course of the next hour, while we prayed that

our bush pilot would come back for us—while they prayed, harder, that their flight to Yellowknife would materialize—the returning veterans recounted what was, generously speaking, a disappointing week.

The camp, when they arrived, was not set up. Several pieces of equipment (including the water pump) didn't work.

It turned out that the gentleman from New South Wales wasn't supposed to be in the camp at all. He'd signed up for a wilderness canoe trip that more or less imploded. He and the other registered canoeists (plus their river guide, Jaime) languished in K. for several days waiting for a plane to pick them up. Finally despairing, a majority of the group contacted another wilderness outfitter back in Yellowknife and organized a river trip of their own, inviting the man from New South Wales (who declined for lack of funds) as well as Jaime (who declined out of loyalty to the employer he'd yet to meet) to join them.

That employer would be EA. Jaime, who—despite his youthful twenty-four years—is a capable and experienced guide, is a native of New Zealand. But he'd never been to EA's camp, never set foot in this part of Canada, and had no experience with the river he was supposed to be guiding on.

When a bush plane finally arrived in K., the two orphaned survivors of the scuttled canoe trip became, respectively, a camp patron and a camp naturalist, joining the trio who were registered for the camp.

They saw no muskox. They saw no caribou. They saw no adult wolves. *But*, on the last day of their trip, they did find two wolf pups.

Jaime, who looks like a cross between Leonardo DiCaprio

and Bob Dylan, found them on an esker about one and a half hours by pontoon boat north of camp.

Esker Al?

"I never saw him leave the camp," the man from New South Wales advised, noting, also, that his health was poor and that he smoked more or less constantly. Judging from the concentration of cigarette butts around the immediate camp, and their absence beyond, I later concluded EA's smoking habit, and limited range, were accurate as described.

None of this was particularly good news. But, I reasoned, the disappointment from having seen little wildlife had probably tarnished their experience. And EA had said to us that the second week was more conducive to seeing caribou. And, I reasoned, it was possible the foursome had come with unreasonable expectations. This was, after all, the Arctic.

And we'd already done everything there was to do in K.— twice. Staying didn't seem to be an attractive option. As for bagging it and just heading home . . .

It's a little bit like playing poker when all your money is sitting in the middle of the table and you're holding a weak hand. You can cut your losses and fold or keep your fingers crossed and stay in the game.

We were glad to hear the sound of our plane returning. Almost as much as the outgoing veterans were thrilled to hear theirs. Two minutes after takeoff, our pontoon plane was skirting over a landscape little changed in seven thousand years. Taiga forest, broken by glacial-ground granite domes and myriads of lakes filled with fossil water. The Canadian Shield, the underlying bedrock that supports much of what is called Canada, ranks among the oldest rock formations on the surface of the planet, some of it dating back 4.5 *billion* years. The taiga forest represents one of the planet's newest habitats—one that grew up in the wake of the last glacier's retreat.

Half an hour out of K., the forest began to lose its uniformity. Soon thereafter, trees drawn more and more into isolated pockets became the vegetative exception instead of the norm. Forty-five minutes into our flight, we were over tundra, the planet's wettest desert. Fifteen minutes later, our pilot began the banking descent that placed us, after a soft splash, brief glide, and short taxi, on the coarse sand beach and the camp of Esker Al.

An Esker Runs Through It

We were prepared to be unimpressed, so therefore were not. The camp was as advertised—a camp. It wasn't a resort. It wasn't a lodge. It was simply a camp whose centerpiece was a large prefab, fabric-and-steel-frame Quonset hut that served as dining room, meeting room, lounge, and library. Designed to house large vehicles and earthmoving equipment, it was light and airy, and offered relief from the wind (which was incessant), the sand (which got into everything), and the biting insects (which dominated the landscape when the wind did not).

More on that later.

Our tents were sturdy and roomy, and the zippered mosquito-net doors worked. The two-by-four and plywood bunks supporting foam rubber cut to fit *might* have been a tad narrow (you learned after a single fall to the floor to use caution when turning over on your side). Overlaid with Therm-a-Rest pads, they were comfortable enough.

The outhouses were . . . well, they were outhouses. The

washroom and shower proved very welcome once the pump got fixed. There was a dock. A couple of skiffs. One pontoon boat. The only other building was a wooden structure with a tarpaper roof north of camp that sported two satellite dishes, a radio antenna, some artwork on the side, an emblem on the front, and a fifteen-year-old wolf-dog named Jake, who moved timidly about the camp and looked as though he could die any second. He did not and I will be eternally grateful for this. The building, guarded by Jake, served as a combination headquarters, staff bunkhouse, and lair of Esker Al.

We picked up our gear on the beach. Exchanged greetings with an imposingly large gentleman who coughed his way through an introduction and who seemed, by process of elimination, to be Esker Al. Learning that our tent was the one on the end, we walked past the hunched figure on the beach trying to reconstruct a water pump.

He and his brother, both from Newfoundland, served as the camp handymen. We met Jaime, the canoe-guide-turned-camp-naturalist, in the kitchen.

Dinner, enjoyed barracks style, was served shortly after we stowed our gear, and it was then that I had my first opportunity to take the measure of our host, and the camp's owner-operator, Esker Al.

A MAN AND HIS SANDCASTLE

One of the things I have noticed throughout my life is how often I have preformulated impressions of people I have never met and how often I am wrong. Not this time. EA was just about the way I'd pictured him.

He was big in almost every respect but distinguished by a head that was the size and shape of a modest-size watermelon and a midsection that attested to a healthy affinity for vict-uals. His eyes, set close and forward, were pale. His hair—gray and thinning—was swept back. He looked, in fact he even sounded a bit, like Ernest Borgnine.

If EA and his camp were made into a movie, I'm sure Er-nest Borgnine would be asked to play the part.

EA wore shorts and a T-shirt that about half covered his midsection, and he went barefoot. He stomped when he walked, jiggled his right knee when he sat, and punctuated many of his pronouncements with a loud, smoker-harsh belly laugh that sounded exactly like he was enunciating the words: "Ha. Ha. Ha."

I think he is the only man I ever met whose laugh was so onomatopoeically apt.

He liked the spotlight. Tried, early on, to engage us with readings from select books treating the north country but gave up when he diagnosed that English, for more than half our group, was less than a second language.

He was not well. He allowed, and I'd already learned, that he was getting over a bout with pneumonia. Insofar as his seemed to be a one-person operation, it explained, at least in part, the communication shortcomings we'd experienced be-fore our arrival. Nevertheless, he smoked two packs of ciga-rettes a day, and if these were not the source of his hacking cough, they didn't help it.

I guessed that he was in his mid-sixties. I was told later, by Terry, that he was, in fact, ten years younger, my age exactly. By the state of the man, by the state of his enterprise, and by his own admission to me one day, he was seeing the end of his days in the camp, and he was looking for a way out.

His client base, he allowed, was dwindling. One hundred and forty-five registrants the previous year, so far fewer than fifty this.

His expenses were going up. He'd been forced to divest himself of the spotter plane advertised in the literature. Prices for everything were being driven up by the mining companies (and the quest for gold and diamonds that was stoking the territory's economy).

He was competing in a global ecotourism market, and the profit margin, never lavish to begin with, was getting finer all the time.

He told me that he hoped Terry, with several business partners, would buy the camp and that they were, in fact, in discussion. There were tears in his eyes.

He told me all these things on our third day at the camp while I was transcribing notes, and this is, perhaps, the most telling evidence attesting to the state of EA's camp and mind. That the owner and operator of a tour company would sit down with a client and openly discuss his financial problems, poor health, declining prospects, and ambition to divest himself of the camp and its obligations. Our conversation ended when EA was overcome by a coughing fit and had to excuse himself.

Yep. Linda and I had hitched our car to somebody else's railroad all right. One that seemed set on pulling up track and whose boiler was fast losing steam. Our only hope was that efforts to find the caribou herd would somehow be successful. There was, we were told by Terry, a spotter plane scheduled to come in on Wednesday. There were plans for a spike camp that some of the group would be in on, but some would not.

We were, after all, in it for the caribou. This effort, as far as we were concerned, lived or died by caribou.

"So, what do you think?" Linda asked as we went to bed that first night.

"I think," I said, "that we keep our fingers crossed and make the most of it."

I don't know what Linda thought. Or maybe I did know and I was just afraid to ask.

Autumn Closin' In

Okay. I'll admit it. I was afraid to ask. I was afraid to ask because, when you are in the Arctic, and things start rolling wrong, they usually continue that way, getting wronger and wronger until the ball stops rolling and your ambitions are frustrated, or you go broke, or you become dead. The Arctic is not a nurturing environment for hope, and it is fatal to most men's dreams. In fact, the Arctic is paved with the bones of explorers, adventurers, gold seekers, and people who pushed the envelope just a bit too far.

On the wall of the Quonset hut, just above the bookshelf and below an assortment of curios, is a photo taken in 1975 showing a bunch of people, mostly seated in front of a wall tent, eating what is probably dinner. During our conversation in the mess hall, EA took it from the wall and placed it in my hands. It evidently meant a lot to him.

The photo was taken on another esker that is visible across the lake. It is named after one of the men in the photo, an archaeologist who, along with his wife and colleagues, exhumed more than ten thousand Native artifacts from the site—a crossing place for migrating caribou and, of course, a place to slaughter them as they swam across the narrows. Peril and safety are as proximally joined as life and death hereabouts.

Propped up in the left-hand corner of the photo is a tall, fit man in his early twenties wearing jeans, work boots, a classically black-and-white-checkered shirt, and a weathered brown hat that must have broken his heart the day he lost it. The man is Esker Al. He is wearing hair that is sixties-era long and a short reddish beard. He is looking at the toes of his boots in a contemplative manner, and in the picture you can find four of the elements that would figure prominently in his life.

In his right hand is a comestible item. In his left, a cigarette. Under his butt is a mound of glacial sand, and around him a group of people who had come into the wilderness to satisfy some ambition. If not then, then soon before or soon thereafter, EA came to the realization that there was a band of the human spectrum eager to engage a corner of the world that was close to his heart and that a career might be made facilitating that interest. While the process of discovery is speculative, the truth and reality are not. By the time of our meeting, EA had been guiding what we now call "ecotourists" for most of his life. Using whatever means and talents he had to spin an eco-dynasty out of dreams. It had commanded his life. It had morphed into his identity.

And now he was approaching the end of his career.

A man does not just wake up one morning and realize that his life has turned the corner, that he's shot his bolt. I'm not speaking about EA now. In fact, I might be speaking about myself. Because, by some curious fate, my life and EA's are similar. Both of us set out at about the same age to make careers out of bringing people and the environment together. EA through outfitting, I through directing the operations of the Cape May Bird Observatory. Both of us pretty much built our institutions from scratch. Both of us committed our lives to the ambition. Both of us have reached the realization that our efforts have brought us precisely *here,* that the future is no more yielding than it was before, and that the horizon never seems to get any closer.

You can't go back. Live the challenges and savor the satisfactions again. Life doesn't move in that direction.

You can move forward. But with what and for what? You don't think like this when you are studying your toes or chewing the end of a pencil at the age of twenty-five. You do at fifty-five.

No, a man doesn't just wake up one morning and realize that he has entered the downside of his life. The jump-off point for "the golden years" that Realtors in places like Florida and Arizona speak of. It's a realization that comes by slow degrees, an identity-dampening elixir whose ingredients are compounded over time.

It begins with small things that bounce off the armor of our self-esteem. The realization that you are now twenty-six. Past the cutoff age for an appointment to West Point or Annapolis. You never wanted a career in the military. But the very fact that you can't have one now undermines the boast that lies in every man's heart that "I can do anything I want to do."

Except now you can't.

Aw, what the heck. Crack another brewski. Here's to twenty-six and being young.

It might surface innocently enough a year or two after you are married. To the girl of your dreams (of course). And you look in the mirror one morning (the same mirror you've been using for years) and see a body . . . but it's not your body (at least not the body you remember). And it's on you!

You step on the scale and see the needle peg a number you didn't even realize lived on the dial.

Your first impulse is: "I've got to do something about that." But after a day or two of salads at lunch and a couple of early morning trips to the gym, it's back to a burger and fries and catching the 7:20 at the station because you really need the sleep.

Oh, what the heck. The girl of your dreams is putting on a few extra ounces, too. It just comes with . . .

It really hits you one day at the height of your career. You, the golden boy. Salesman of the year back in . . . The one all the companies were pursuing. The one whose greatest challenge had always been determining the best career choice but who has just been presented with a new, out-of-the-blue choice: move yourself and your family to the other side of the country or lose your job.

You! The person who was always in control of his destiny discovers that it is "the organization" and "circumstances" that are destiny brokers now.

Then comes the day you get the call from one of your old high school friends . . .

"Phil? I can't believe it. Oh, man, it's been ages. You know just the other day I was . . ."

"No, I haven't heard."

"Oh no. You're kidding! When? Oh, that can't be. I mean, didn't he have checkups? There're tests they do for . . . I can't believe . . . I mean, he was only . . ."

He was your age, exactly. You graduated in the same class.

The next day, at the lunch counter, over your burger and fries, you pick up a discarded newspaper. You flip to the obituaries. Start going through the names, but what you are interested in is ages, and what you discover, with a start, is that a lot of the poor stiffs they're writing about aren't old, like your father (rest his soul). A lot of them are young. Like you! Except they are dead.

Bad luck, you think. Or maybe they just weren't careful or as health conscious as . . .

Finding it more difficult to do all the things you used to do now. Straightening up the garage. Pulling the boat out of the water at the end of the season. Walking the dog all the way to the end of the street.

You start paying kids to do chores. When you have a flat tire, you call a tow service instead of changing it yourself (don't even know where they hide the jacks on vehicles these days).

When you board a plane, the girl in the next seat doesn't even return your smile before burying her face in a book and pulling her elbows in. And more and more when you call your old clients, there's a new voice at that extension, who has a conference call in just a few minutes and asks you to "just send an e-mail stating your business."

And when your boss retires, the person who gets the job isn't you! It's the snotty kid who's half your age who got it only (you're sure) because he's the one everyone calls when their computer gets cranky.

Including you.

You toy with the idea of retirement—but you know you aren't there yet, not financially. Should have started socking it away sooner. Should have bought that place on the lake back when prices were . . .

It was something you always just assumed you'd have someday. You know. Your dreams.

It was something that was just assured. Like lasting love. Providing you worked hard for it, put your heart in it.

Isn't that the way life was supposed to be?

So now here you are. With your dreams unrealized, and all you have to show is all you have to show.

It is a purely human affliction to be blessed or cursed by dreams and to measure the success or failure of our lives by them. But instead of bemoaning fate, we humans might do well to count our blessings. In many places, the Arctic among them, most things don't live long enough to pursue dreams. In the Arctic, most things run to stay just ahead of nightmares.

SOPHIE'S CHOICE

She entered the Quonset hut and pulled off her mosquito-net hat, disclosing a long, thin face framed by dark hair, features that were sharp and fine, and eyes that exuded intelligence and compassion. Her name was Sophie. She was a thirty-one-year-old French biologist, specializing in bear reintroduction and blue tits, chickadee-like birds that are widespread in Europe.

She was here, like her photographer friend, Jacques, to study wolves. Since our arrival, it was a rare moment when one or both of them were not seated on the hill above the esker den site, watching, hoping, because biologists have dreams, too (although they might call them hypotheses and disguise them as questions).

It was the middle of the afternoon, and somehow I doubted that it was the swarming mosquitoes and black flies that had driven Sophie in. She might have been slight unto frail. Squashed insects and all, I doubt she topped the scale at ninety pounds—in part because she was naturally small-framed. But in no small part because Sophie was a strict vegetarian. More than once I saw her eschew all the offerings on the table except those that were housed in the salad bowl. When packing lunches for all-day outings, Sophie ignored the sandwich fixings and stuffed a lock-top bag with lettuce.

But vegetarian or no, she was as single-mindedly determined as any predator with regard to her quarry, so I doubted it was insects that had made her quit. My guess was that it was the mounting futility that had driven her to abandon her vigil above the den, and it might have been she was motivated by more than this. A nightmare, and a recurring one. It even has a name. It is called "the struggle for life and death in the Arctic." Scientists, being scientists, accept this. But many, perhaps most, scientists, being human, are not unmoved by it.

"Anything?" I asked, because, since she was a dedicated academician, there was a good chance Sophie would bury herself in a book before realizing I was there and interested in the fruits of her observations.

"Ehh'no," she said in tones that matched the hurt in her eyes. "Nothing," she added with the finality of a last breath.

"The pup?" I hoped more than asked. Surely she'd seen the wolf pup.

"Nothing," she said again and then paused. Mustering her English to fill in the blanks. "We theenk, maybe eet is in thee den. We theenk, maybe, it is not do good."

"Theenk, maybe" means "hope." "Not do good" means "it starves."

I nodded. That was why I had chosen not to visit the den site myself. The pup had not been seen for two days now, and after five days there was still no sign of the adult wolves—hadn't been any sightings since the female that first night.

The pup had made his appearance on the second day amid great excitement. A gray animal, fairly advanced, maybe twelve weeks old. Over the course of one day and the next, he moved about the area in front of the den—a large, dark portal framed by tree roots. There were other entrances, but as time went on it became increasingly clear that there was only one pup. This is unusual. Females commonly give birth to four or five. Until about eight to ten weeks of age, they are nourished by the milk of their mother, who remains vigilantly close to the den. After that, they, and increasingly she, are dependent upon food brought to the den by the male, who carries it in his stomach and regurgitates upon delivery.

The food, of course, is meat. The meat of choice is caribou, and that, of course, was the problem. A recurring problem in this corner of the Arctic. A nightmare. The movement of caribou is unpredictable. Their presence is allied more to a possibility than to a promise. As already noted, the animals leave the edge of the taiga in April and head for calving areas near the coast—for some a distance exceeding five hundred miles. The return begins in late June and early July, but it lacks urgency and direction. There is no reason to reach the tree line until October, when the rut, mating time, occurs.

All along the return route there are wolves with young mouths to feed and hungry bellies of their own. With young confined to dens, adult wolves cannot follow the caribou. With most of the tundra dominated by paw-resistant permafrost, the wolves are forced to den in places where the substrate is not locked in permanent ice—along south-facing riverbanks and, especially, on eskers, whose sandy, percolation-enhanced substrate is permafrost-proof and easy to excavate.

The wolves are tied to the eskers, and their breeding success is tied to one very risky gambit. That the caribou migration *this* year will pass close enough to *their* den sites to provide food for the pups before they starve.

In good years, those in which the southbound herd moves close and on time, breeding success is good. In years when fate turns its back on wolves, the male will work to stave off starvation by bringing in smaller and less energetically advantaged prey—hares, ptarmigan, waterfowl, even lemmings. But hares and lemmings and ptarmigan populations are cyclic. Waterfowl are difficult to catch. When secondary prey numbers, too, are low, hunting success goes down, and even territories covering hundreds of square miles are not enough to meet the needs of growing wolves.

Locally, this seemed to be one of those years. In five days, Linda and I had seen precisely two willow ptarmigan. We'd seen exactly no lemmings, and we saw few bird species that commonly feed on lemmings—no rough-legged hawks and only a handful of parasitic jaegers.

But all the evidence we needed in order to see how life was shaking out in the Barren Lands in July 2007 could be found at the entrance to the wolf den. A single surviving pup from what was probably a litter of four or five. No adults to be seen. Father, off hunting or perhaps dead. Mother, in desperation, hunting, too.

The pup? A single animal deprived of littermates moving sluggishly about the area of the den? What do you think? It's an honest question because, frankly, your guess is as good as mine. "I think I'll go up to the den," I announced to Sophie, without much thought and with even less optimism. Heck. It beat sitting inside.

It was about a twenty-five-minute walk to the top of the hill where the den was viewed. If you pushed it, if the bugs were bad, you could do it in fifteen to twenty, and the bugs, black flies, were bad. The winds were light and somewhat northerly, blowing toward the den, which, from the standpoint of watching wildlife, is not a good thing. But the hill was a couple of hundred feet above the valley floor, and the sun-heated earth would ensure that my scent would carry over the den site. No, my scent wouldn't be a problem.

There was no one else around and, as Sophie had said, no sign of the pup at the den. I raised my binoculars, starting a scan of the open sand, searching for tracks, when I heard the sound of someone approaching and, turning, was surprised to see Sophie, who sat down to join me.

Apparently, she'd concluded that the slim chance of seeing a wolf that being outside afforded beat the no chance that being inside ensured.

We sat in silence. Her English was passable but effortful. What little I'd gleaned from my single year of high school French didn't survive past graduation. Sophie and I had spoken sparingly during the week, and most of our interactions had revolved around birds. Whenever I spotted a new species, and Sophie was in the vicinity, I made it a point to bring it to her attention. But conversations?

Scant unto nil.

Under these circumstances, small talk is no less effortful than big talk—meaning discussion relating to personal convictions as opposed to "Where did you get your degree?" and "How did you meet Jacques?" And there was one question that was really eating me. I was really curious to know how a person who was a vegetarian could be so fascinated by one of the world's most consummate predators. An animal that likes its meat so fresh it sometimes doesn't bother to end its victim's life before eating it.

So I moved the question for discussion.

"You don't eat meat?"

"No," she replied. If she was taken aback by the directness of the question, it didn't show in the directness of her reply, and it didn't show in her eyes—but there was a reason for this. Behind the mosquito netting, I couldn't see Sophie's eyes.

"Is it for health or for conviction?" I asked, knowing as soon as I said it that it was too obliquely stated, so I rephrased the question. "To feel good, healthy? Or for ethics? Concern?" I said, hoping I wasn't putting words into her mouth, hoping she got my meaning. She did.

"It is for the poor animals," she said. She shook her head, side to side, to underline the strength of her conviction. "I work . . . I *volunteer* sometimes," she corrected, "for organizations that protect animals."

Well, that answered that. Not only was Sophie a vegetarian but her dietary discipline was linked to a desire not to inflict hurt or harm upon animals. Sophie *cared* about animals. And she put her mouth, and the rest of her digestive tract, where her convictions were.

I have a great respect for this. First, because I think that people who choose to limit their biofootprint are being responsible citizens of the planet—backing up sound ethics and understanding with calculated reserve. Second, because, like Sophie, I too care about animals and am committed to their protection. I work for the New Jersey Audubon Society. I've spent my life striving to safeguard the marvelous and complex diversity that constitutes the natural world.

The difference between Sophie and me is that not only am I a meat eater but I am a hunter. We have much the same ambitions. To be caring and responsible custodians of the planet and its denizens. We've chosen different avenues.

She by becoming a primary consumer, eating lower down on the trophic ladder. I by bypassing the mass-production industry of animal husbandry, slaughter, packaging, and shipping, and getting my food, as much as possible, direct from nature—cutting out the middlemen, bypassing an energy-consumptive and morally buffering system that reduces humans from predators to carrion feeders.

Sorry if this shocks you. But if you went to a store today and picked up a pound of ground round or pork tenderloin antiseptically wrapped and FDA-approved, then you are a consumer of meat from an animal that was killed by somebody else.

That meets the definition of a carrion feeder.

I'm a carrion feeder, too (as, in fact, are most meat-eating animals at need). But my preference, my conviction, arrived at by both awareness and conscious choice, is to hunt for the meat Linda and I consume. I hunt deer every fall. They are, now, a common element in the tapestry that is New Jersey's environment. I try to kill at least two, three if I can. Three deer is just a little more than Linda and I can consume over the course of a year and just a little less than the demand from coworkers and friends who want a share of the spoils.

Members of my immediate pack.

I find, when I sit down to a meal of grilled venison chops, supported with vegetables purchased from the local farm-stand two miles from our home, that I feel just a little bit better about my place on this planet. I feel a little more honest and a little more directly connected and a lot more ethical at such times than I do when I'm eating out of the store.

I feel, I am sure, much like Sophie and other people who care about animals and who forge their caring into conviction. And I often try to convey the scope of the common ground that underlies both hunting and the vegetarian life-style—to both hunters and nonhunters alike—usually with success. Because when it comes to supporting opinions, there is nothing more convincing than the truth.

All of this was a lot to try to convey to Sophie, knowing our linguistic limits and not knowing the strength or philosophical underpinnings of her convictions beyond the fact that she cared about animals. Still, she was a scientist—a discipline anchored in objective analysis and strengthened by the challenge of peers to any and all conclusions. And she was here to study an animal that was the very antithesis of a vegetarian lifestyle. So I decided to be bold. Wolfish.

"I'm a hunter," I announced. "For deer, which are common where I live. Linda and I eat them."

I'm not sure what kind of response I expected. Some measure of disapproval, I suppose. Some degree of incomprehension that would command more explanation than our linguistic limitation could accommodate.

What I did not expect was a question that cut right through the fabric of our common ground, down to the very foundation of hunting.

"Do you respect the animals you kill?" she said, turning her veiled face toward me. And I would have given anything to have seen, at that moment, the eyes of the person who could have formulated a question so penetrating.

I felt momentarily shaken. Felt like a wolf that was just trotting along, minding his own business, and suddenly found himself on the ground with a caribou's jaws tightening over his throat. This person, this nonhunter, in a simple question, had not only defined the thing that makes the taking of life sanctionable but put my convictions on trial.

I wanted to tell her how central the matter of respect is to me—how I believe that respect is the moral foundation of hunting. Without it, hunting is just killing animals.

I wanted to tell her how much care I lavish on preparations before I hunt. How much time I spend shooting on the range so that my skill is equal to my obligation as a hunter. How much attention I pay to the place I will hunt—choosing a location that will offer not only a clear and open shot but time to assess and plan that shot. So that it will not be rushed. So that I will not make mistakes.

And I wanted to tell her that after the shot, with an animal now flush with the earth and the universe accommodating this sudden shift in the balance between life and death, I recount in my mind all the elements of the drama that just unfolded so that the deer, which will become part of my body, will also live in my mind for as long as thoughts dwell there.

I wanted to tell Sophie these things, realizing then that these are things I have never even told another hunter. So instead I answered her most poignant of questions with the most direct of answers. A response as honest and accurate as a single shot.

"Yes," I said.

"That is good," she said, turning her binoculars once more upon the den site. "So long as you respect."

I wish that all vegetarians had the wisdom Sophie commands. Hunters, too.

We stayed another twenty minutes, surrendering, finally, to the lure of dinner and the ferocity of the black flies. The pup never appeared. Not then, or ever. And two days later, when we walked up on the den site after a night of rain, we found no track—of any size.

"Maybe there is another den?" Sophie said, voicing the hope that lived in all of us. And maybe there was. On another esker, not this one. But while the Barren Lands are a very big place, there is remarkably little room for "maybe." We were going to get a lesson in that, too.

Where the Caribou Weren't

As it turned out the plane that was supposed to arrive on Wednesday was abruptly rescheduled for late Thursday, but by this time we weren't surprised. Our sole effort to find caribou would be delayed until Friday, the day before we were to leave. The spike camp, whose organization had commanded most of Terry's time on Tuesday, was canceled. Without any knowledge concerning the whereabouts of the herd, there was no practical reason to just strike out into the wilderness.

In the end, we were left to rely upon two slim pieces of intelligence. That one week ago, the caribou had been seen near lake X and that so far they had not reached fishing lodge Y.

They were, presumably, but with no assurance, somewhere in between. The only other advantage we had was EA's "four decades of traditional guiding knowledge."

Terry summarized our chances this way: "It's like looking for a needle in a haystack."

"Isn't this the situation we spent all this money in order to avoid?" Linda asked.

"What," I said, feigning surprise I hardly felt, "you don't have any faith in 'nearly four decades of traditional guiding knowledge'?"

"Oh, I do," Linda assured. "And I note that 'nearly four decades of traditional guiding knowledge' isn't going with us." It was Terry who was assigned the task of flying with the group. Throughout the morning, EA had been conspicuously absent.

"On the radio," we were told. "Trying all his contacts to get some up-to-the-minute information on the herd."

Still, there was a slim chance that our plane would intersect the herd and, if not the main herd, then elements of the herd. And if we didn't hit the herd directly, then there was a chance that we'd cross their path. Among the remarkable features of tundra, as seen from the air, are the myriad caribou trails that crease the vegetative patchwork. You can see them from the ground, of course, most commonly as a series of parallel rivulets climbing hillsides. But from the air you can see not scores but hundreds of paths, scored into earth, fanning out across open plains and coalescing in ridgetop saddles and at constricted crossing points across lakes.

Old trails, going back many years, look like pale scars. Fresh trails appear darkly ragged, the vegetation recently chewed. If we saw fresh trails, we'd know we were behind the herd and finding them was just a matter of following the tracks until we caught up (or had to turn around for lack of fuel). There was certainly a chance.

Heck, wolves have been pinning their survival on just heading out into the Barren Lands and intersecting the caribou for generations, and wolves don't have spotter planes either.

We lifted off just before noon and climbed to an altitude of about five hundred feet, heading northwest.

We traveled in that direction for an hour, crossing a landscape that measures time in seasons and the epochal advance and retreat of ice.

THE BARREN LANDS

We were once again in a de Havilland Otter. This one looked to be about forty years old—but then just about everything that ferries people and gear around the Arctic looks to be about forty years old (even after a single summer's service).

Five hundred feet is a fine altitude for spotting large ungulates, and it's not so high that even things as small as large birds go undetected. On the many lakes we overflew, small flocks of Canada geese churned across the water in response to our approach. Every so often a ptarmigan would flush, and occasionally the dark blue backdrop of a lake would frame the sliver-winged profile of a herring gull.

But the caribou that we so much wanted to see were absent or, more accurately, not to be found along the narrow slice of the Barren Lands sampled by our plane. They most certainly were here. They just weren't where we looked. And this failure, far more than any accident of success, says something about this corner of the world that is easy to express but very hard for most people to comprehend.

It is vast. Vast enough to swallow the million-plus Barren

Ground caribou living in Canada and have vastness to spare. Vast enough that, three hundred years after the first European dared venture into this place, it remains virtually unchallenged and unchanged.

The last great wilderness left on Earth.

I invite you to think about this a moment. Think about what this means. Think about this whole big planet, whose tallest peaks, deepest submarine canyons, driest deserts, densest forests, have been climbed, crossed, plumbed, and then chronicled in the pages of *National Geographic* magazine.

In 1805, Lewis and Clark stood on the shore of the Pacific Ocean. In 1880 the United States Census Bureau declared the American Frontier gone. In 1916 the Trans-Siberian Railroad was completed. In your lifetime, the last Stone Age peoples were discovered in the Amazon Basin and the forests of New Guinea. In 1958 the *USS Nautilus* sailed beneath the polar icecap. In 1961 the first human penetrated the outer limits of the earth's atmosphere and entered space. In 2011 the population of the earth was nearly 7 billion people.

Yet in the Barren Lands of northwest Canada, there are thousands of square miles where nobody lives or has lived since the ice surrendered its grip seven thousand years ago.

Nobody. Humans visit. People don't live there.

Not the Dene people who in the summer travel north from their villages at the edge of the great boreal forest to catch fish in the mosaic of still-unnamed lakes or to ambush caribou herds before winter sends the hunters and the hunted back to the shelter of the trees.

Not the Inuit, who pursue the caribou from the north but in winter withdraw to the relative comfort and safety of the coast, where the ocean still supports animals to hunt and temperatures are tempered by the unfreezing water beneath the seasonal cap of ice.

Not the trappers, who for a brief span of years eked out a living in roughed-out cabins situated on the eskers but whose fortitude, in this age of fur farming and environmental consciousness, is now largely bereft of fortune. Not the geologists, who buzz about the barrens in helicopters and floatplanes in search of samples and survey data but who retreat into laboratories to analyze samples and write their reports when the air reaches temperatures that turn propane to jelly in the tank and freeze exposed skin to metal on contact.

And in the summer, the insects make the place a living hell for anything that bleeds.

One of the last, few, great unpeopled wildernesses on Earth. A vessel big enough to swallow caribou and aspirations and leave no trace.

After an hour's flight time, we descended and landed on a lake flanked, of course, by an esker. An hour later we were back in the air, heading north, then turning southeast, homebound but on a course that would put us over new ground.

Barren ground. Barren Land. Once again, no sign of the herd. Like the wolf pup back at the esker, our effort starved.

ESKER AFTERMATH

It was early, early by the midnight-sun-calibrated standards of Yellowknife residents anyway. Linda and I had the lounge in the plush new motel in diamond-driven Yellowknife all to ourselves.

We were drinking wine—first, because at the happy hour rate of seven dollars a glass it was the cheapest alcohol in the establishment. Second, because in Yellowknife, when you order a martini, its alcoholic core is one measured fluid ounce.

That's not a martini. That's an insult to an olive.

"Cheers," I said, raising my glass.

"Cheers," she intoned. Catching and holding my eyes with hers. Tired eyes.

It had taken pretty nearly all day to get from EA's camp back to Yellowknife. We'd caught the second of two shuttles back to K. (having informed the pilot that if he stranded us we'd hunt him down and dismember him, only to learn that another member of our party had already made a similar threat and we stood second in line). Our flight to Yellowknife was on time. We took a shuttle to the motel. Checked in. Showered. Then headed down to the lounge to decide about dinner. Neither of us was particularly hungry.

"I guess that was a waste," Linda said.

"Not entirely," I countered. "We got to see some new country, new habitat. You got a few good shots, and I've got some copy."

"No caribou," she said, cutting right to the chase. "It's not the story we wanted."

"No caribou," I agreed. "Different story. Maybe a better story; more honest."

"We left all those caribou on the Teshekpuk and flew out here and saw *nothing!*" she said, choking on the disappointment.

"Could be worse," I offered.

"Yeah, we could *still* be out there and *still* seeing nothing."

In the end, we skipped dinner (but we sure as hell did have another glass of wine). And in the morning, when we caught our flight out, we changed our itinerary—heading to California for a few days, to visit Linda's folks, and not directly back to Alaska as planned.

We decided, after our disappointing experience, we needed a break.

Esker Al? Oh, he's still out there, I guess. Still running his dreams to ground in the Barren Lands.

And the caribou? They're still out there, too.

Where?

That's the perennial question, isn't it?

Note to readers: Nobody after reading this chapter should be dissuaded from engaging the services of the many fine Canadian and Alaskan lodges and tour operators whose privilege it is to open the doors to Arctic visitors. Trips that exceed expectations are the norm; trips that fall short are no more (and probably less) likely than any other travel option.

Just bring lots of reading material (and don't forget the bug spray).

CHAPTER 5

Moon Month of Akullirut (August–September),
"Caribou Hair Thickens"

Bob and Lisa and Linda and Pete's Most Excellent Trip to the John

Gates of the Arctic National Park, Alaska

DAY 1, SUNDAY, AUGUST 12, 2007

"Is it ringing now?" the two-way radio in Lisa's hand demanded.

"No," she sighed.

"Now?"

"No."

"How about now?"

"Nooo," she repeated. "Bob, I've got to finish packing the food."

"Now?"

"No."

"Now?"

Bob was beginning to sound exasperated, and not without foundation. The day was young, but the co-owner of Wilderness Birding Adventures had already wasted several hours trying to transfer funds electronically from one account to another (only to be told, repeatedly, that the bank's computers were down for routine maintenance).

This is one of the problems with being an Alaska time zone resident and dealing with bank computers that keep East Coast hours.

The newly discovered systems failure on the electronic dog fence, which had him outside patrolling the perimeter (and Lisa monitoring his failed effort from the inside control panel), was just the latest in a string of stress-elevating snafus sabotaging our scheduled 7:00 A.M. departure for Fairbanks.

You know. The kind of unexpected, last-minute crap that always crops up when someone goes on a really big trip they are really looking forward to.

"Anything we can do to help?" I asked, knowing there wasn't, feeling obligated to ask anyway.

"Noo," Lisa said, throwing me a confidence-instilling smile. The kind of playbook smile backcountry tour operators offer clients when things aren't going well and the last thing anyone in a position of responsibility needs (or wants) is a superfluous hand.

What it showed was how tired our friend was. Packing gear and dealing with a last-minute flurry of e-mail correspondence with clients and contractors, the other co-owner of Wilderness Birding Adventures hadn't gotten to bed until after 2:00 A.M., and had risen at 6:00.

And it was the end of a long season for Lisa. Since April, the burden of organizing flights, handling clients, packing and shipping food, and maneuvering rafts, folding canoes, tents, and other essential backcountry equipment to various drop-off points all over the state had fallen largely upon her slight, lithe, but eminently capable shoulders.

And she was, now, in mid-August, utterly and certifiably fried.

It was easy for me to recognize Lisa's malady. I suffer from it, too. Difficulty shedding the workaday me and surrendering to the great, calming interface that a wilderness experience confers.

Of course, first you have to get away—which, two hours, one deferred financial transaction, one unresolved dog fence malfunction, and a hurried breakfast later, we did.

"I hope the doggies survive," Bob pronounced, as our gear-crammed pickup cleared their drive in Eagle River, heading for Highway 1 and the seven-and-a-half-hour drive north to Fairbanks.

"What time is it?" he growled, but now that we were under way, the growl had lost its bite. In fact, if I wasn't mistaken, there was an underlying purr to his words.

"Just after nine," Linda proclaimed. "No worries."

Linda was already in vaca mode, already slipping into Arctic time.

"Not too bad," I said, turning, flashing what I hoped was a convincing smile. Fact is, I'm in the Vince Lombardi school when it comes to schedules. If you aren't early, you're late. I'm early even for dentist appointments.

But now that we were finally on the road, I was relaxing, too. Lisa?

Her forehead still furrowed, Lisa was doing a last-minute rundown of the to do list in her hand. A long list. Filled with items that could make the difference between having a good trip and having a bad one.

"The only thing not crossed off is bear spray," she announced, and with that utterance, Lisa Moorehead, tour operator, disappeared and Lisa-heading-into-the-Arctic took her place. She leaned back in the seat. Put the list away. Smiled.

It's not that bear spray wasn't an important item. It's just that, as all of us knew, the needed canisters of *Ursus*-calibrated pepper spray were waiting for us at the Wright Air Service counter in Fairbanks. Wright was our carrier to the village of Bettles, gateway to the Gates of the Arctic National Park, where our river trip would start.

What Lisa's pronouncement had certified was that all the planning and doing was done. The die was cast. Let the fun begin.

"Tunes," Linda "the Tunester" Dunne demanded.

"Awwwl right," Bob rumbled, reaching for the CD holder, feeding a shiny disk into the player. Ramping the volume to middle-aged-ear-accommodating levels.

While I'm not the world's biggest Beatles fan, I must admit that a more appropriate collection could hardly have been found to accompany four friends, all drawn from the ranks of the baby-boomer generation, heading off on a long-anticipated adventure together.

We foot-tapped and dashboard-thumped our way through "Lucy in the Sky with Diamonds," sang backup to "Hey Jude," and lapsed into soulful silence under the spell of "Norwegian Wood."

We discussed where we were in the then short span of our

lives when the "White Album" was released, then what we were doing when we heard that John Lennon had been shot. When, for one soul-shuddering moment, the generation that had vowed it would "die before it got old" felt its mortality.

As the peaks of the Alaska Range came more and more to fill the windshield, we talked gaily about old friends . . .

And have you heard from . . .

And did you know that . . .

We discussed where to stop and get a latte.

And laughed about that time, on the Kongakut, when we saw the wolves.

And recalled those Thanksgiving weekend parties up in Westline, Pennsylvania, that didn't really get going until the bar was legally closed . . .

Seven and a half hours goes quickly when three decades of friendship goes along for the ride. It was raining, lightly, when we reached the outskirts of Fairbanks. The air was chill. The fireweed beside the road had already shed most of its blossoms.

We turned on NPR and learned, among other things, that a computer glitch had stranded forty thousand passengers at LAX, many aboard planes.

Not our problem. No longer our world.

DAY 2, MONDAY, AUGUST 13
The next morning, after a traditional last morning "in town" breakfast at Sam's Sourdough Cafe, we rolled up to the weigh-in counter at Wright Air to get the bad news.

Our combined weight, four humans plus gear, was 1,350 pounds—about 250 pounds over budget.

We'd be fine for the first leg of our trip, Fairbanks to Bettles.

But the single-engine Beaver we'd chartered to fly us from Bettles to the small lake adjacent to our put-in point on the John River couldn't take us, and all the fixings, in one flight.

It meant trimming gear or paying for two shuttles.

We tried. We shed clothes, food, backup cans of fuel, and camera gear (and a few tears). Even the wine! It was no use.

In the end, we surrendered to the inevitable and ate the expense. Loaded up two planes in Bettles and settled in for the one-and-a-half-hour flight into the stony heart of the Brooks Range. Linda's and my pilot was a likable, baseball-capped, gum-chewing young man named Scott.

"But you can call me by my nickname, Crash," he offered. He didn't even crack a smile when he said it, attesting to the timeworn nature of the line.

As we were taxiing out onto the lake that would serve as our runway, I noticed that the poplars rimming the shore were already touched by the season, splashed, here and there, with yellow. Autumn yellow.

Racing the engine until everything in the plane, from the fuselage to the fillings in our teeth, was rattling, Crash got us airborne and turned north, following the lead plane, which was tracing the course of the river. The river that flowed south out of the Brooks Range. Our river for the next ten days. The John.

It was the Brooks that filled the windshield now. Rust and gray, stark and brittle, softened in places and at best by a thin veneer of vegetation. The Brooks are angry-looking, no-nonsense mountains, geologically young and still pissed at the tectonic plate that disturbed their slumber.

Seven hundred and twenty miles across, separating the

body of Alaska from the North Slope, the Brooks Range is composed, mostly, of layered sedimentary rocks deposited as silt in the warm seas overlying most of northern Alaska during the second half of the Paleozoic and first part of the Mesozoic era, 220 to 370 million years ago. This tranquil period lasted millions of years, but it ended in violence.

Beginning 180 million years ago, about the middle of the Jurassic period, two of the earth's tectonic plates collided, resulting in a great lifting and piling up of the continental crust. Like layers of snow piled up by a snowplow, horizontal layers of sedimentary rock were folded and turned on end. The folding process continued for about 60 million years.

Not particularly high as mountain ranges go—their highest peak, Mount Isto, barely tops nine thousand feet—the part of the Brooks we were heading for was the middle portion, the region mantled by the Endicott Mountains. The headwaters of the John lie close to Anaktuvuk Pass, one of the few access routes, for humans and animals, across the range. The small lake that was our destination and put-in point was about forty miles south of Anaktuvuk, where the John River proper meets the Hunt Fork near the southern boundary of the Gates of the Arctic National Park, the northernmost (and least visited) national park in the United States.

The John, winding its way through the south slope of the Brooks, is bordered by no settlements, and since it is, for most of its length, a tranquil river, it is not as popular as many other Arctic waterways.

This suited us fine.

Two hours later, our gear piled on the shore and the receding hum of the Beavers finally eclipsed by distance, we got down to the business of portaging 750 pounds of gear down to the river and setting up camp for the night.

But not before fortifying ourselves with lunch. Assorted cheeses, hunterstick sausage, and hummus-dipped vegetables topped off with Wilderness Birding Adventures's prize-winning, triple A–rated gorp.

Gorp, in case you are unfamiliar with the term, is a blood-sugar-boosting, artery-constricting blend of assorted nuts and M&M's. It's the kind of temptation you keep in the back of the cupboard and out of sight at home but down by the handful when you are having a wilderness experience and things like cholesterol levels and belt size have no standing.

It was raining lightly, but that was fine. The rain would help keep water levels up and mosquito numbers down.

Day 3, No Date, No Time

We woke late and rose later. In August, the breeding birds that have not already departed greet mornings with sheathed beaks. Family groups are wandering. Territories unraveling. There is no longer any need for males to post notice of occupancy (or eligibility) with song.

I don't know what time we started our day. Still morning judging by the sun that was still east of the river, which runs north–south. Everyday standards of time don't count for much in the wilderness. The concept of a minute is irrelevant, a second incomprehensible. What trumps time is the reality of the moment.

The first thing I do when I step off a bush plane is take off my watch. Throw it in the bottom of my dry bag. From then until the end of the trip, it is day, not date, that matters. We had nine days, now, to get where we were going. When we traveled, how far, and where we chose to lay over were totally up to us.

It had taken most of the previous afternoon to portage our gear from the lake to the river, choose tent sites, and set up the cooking area well away from where we would sleep.

This was bear country, and while the John is not a highly trafficked river, prime put-in sites are known to local bears, and bears who capitalize upon this knowledge (by helping themselves to your food stocks) are, at the very least, a nuisance and, if poorly planned for, a threat.

Keeping food in one place and you in another is a commonsense practice, and storing food in bear-proof containers and/or ringing campsites with electric bear fence is a way of keeping the peace and helping to ensure that a good bear doesn't go bad.

Of course, effective diplomacy is contingent upon the threat of force. Bolstering our efforts to maintain the peace were the aforementioned canisters of bear spray (one per tent/couple) and a twelve-gauge pump capable of discharging a thought-provoking array of discouragement—exploding cracker shells, flares, nonlethal beanbag shells, and, finally, if efforts at diplomacy and tempered displays of force fall short, bear-stopper slugs.

Were we expecting bear trouble? No. If we were expecting trouble, I'd have brought a slug gun of my own and augmented my confidence with a .44 Magnum. We were simply being prudent.

The south slope of the Brooks Range is simply riddled with black bears and grizzly bears, and in August the tundra is one big communal berry patch. The vast majority of bears want nothing more than to be left in peace and, given half a chance, will go more than halfway to avoid an issue with one of our species.

But bears are large and formidable, somewhat used to getting their way. They are also, on occasion, hard to read. Situations sometimes arise that are both accidental and unforeseen. Having something at your disposal that can keep the unexpected from escalating to the unfortunate not only is confidence building but helps you keep a clear head so that you don't do something stupid to make a bad moment worse.

Bob and I have both had occasion to confront bears with weapons in our hands (Bob more times that I). Neither of us has ever been brought to use lethal force.

After a breakfast of omelets so hearty it brought us close to inertia, we (except Lisa, the tea drinker) fortified our resolve with additional cups of French roast coffee and got down to the serious business of putting our two Ally folding canoes together. It was then that we confronted our first major challenge of the trip.

No. Not bears in camp. But certainly something accidental and unforeseen.

"Uh-oh," said Bob, looking down at the array of canoe-building parts piled at his feet. There was enough volume and urgency in the expression to make all of us turn our heads.

"What?" Lisa demanded so quickly she trimmed the one-syllable word by half.

"The bow and stern pieces are missing on this one," he said, and one omelet, five pieces of sausage, and one and a half bagels went into a fusion reaction that exploded in my gut and shot a mushroom cloud of anxiety into the base of my brain.

"Maybetheygot packedwithothercanoe," she suggested.

"I looked," he said.

There followed a period of silence while four disaster-enhanced minds searched furtively for some way out of what was a real dilemma. Although any missing part of the canoe's inner frame was important, the curved bow and stern sections were especially critical. They were, literally, the cutting edge of a craft designed to cut through water. They were also the anchoring points for the vinyl skin that would separate us, and our gear, from the river.

This was much worse than a dog fence on the fritz.

We couldn't do the trip in a single canoe. Too much gear; too many people.

We could, conceivably, fly in the missing parts. Use Bob's satellite phone to call out. Have someone locate the parts from whatever corner of Alaska the balance of WBA's canoe fleet was being stored. Air-ship the parts to Bettles, where we'd have to arrange another bush flight to have them dropped off. It would take money and, worst of all, days.

We could also decide to stay where we were. Take day hikes. Pay for a bush flight out. Put up, now and again, with other parties being flown in.

Bob looked at Lisa. Lisa looked at Bob. The unspoken conversation being transmitted along well-worn spousal airwaves might have gone something like this.

"What are we going to do?"

"I don't know. Figure something out."

"How the [deleted in the name of civility] could this possibly have happened?"

"I'll bet when the canoes were taken apart after the Colville River trip somebody packed the bow pieces in with another canoe."

"Well, why didn't you check the kit before we left?"

"I planned to, but we ran out of time."

"Well, this is just great, Bob. This is really swell."

"Don't worry. We'll figure something out."

"We better figure something out!"

"Don't get mad. That's not going to help."

"I'm not mad. I'm angry and I'm frustrated and I don't want this to be happening."

"We'll figure something out."

"Okay then. I'll be over there watching the Brooks Range wear down while you're figuring it out."

Not far away, another couple with a vested interest in the unfolding dilemma was transmitting their own conversation.

"Well, this really [fill in the blank]."

"Yeah. This really [you guess]."

"Poor Bob. I'll bet he feels terrible."

"Poor Lisa. I'll bet she feels horrible."

"This sure will put the kibosh on this venture if we get stuck here."

"It sure will put a strain on our expedition equanimity if we get stuck here."

"Well, getting all negative isn't going to help the situation."

"Well, projecting your negativity onto me isn't either, bucko."

"Don't worry. We'll figure something out."

"Well, okay then. I'm going to go help Lisa while you two sons of Jack London figure something out."

In short order, Bob and I found ourselves stranded beside a shorted pile of hardware, deep in the process of "figuring something out," which in retrospect strikes me as both amusing and fascinating.

Lisa and Linda are two of the most competent, problem-solving people the evolutionary process has spawned to date. Lisa, a onetime full-time river guide, spent years dealing with things that are supposed to float but too often don't. Linda, daughter of an engineer and the principal fix-it person around household Dunne, is twice the problem solver I am.

Despite their backgrounds and problem-solving attributes, they voluntarily and almost automatically stepped back and left it to the members of the party with the Y chromosomes to figure out.

That's the amusing part. The fascinating thing is that both of us were suddenly so happy with the prospect of having a challenge to resolve that we were actually grinning at each other. You'd almost think Bob had hidden the missing parts.

What's more, and without a spoken word, the Y-chromosome-driven centers of our brains had simultaneously gone down the same neural pathway and come up with near-identical solutions. This should surprise no one with a Y chromosome who grew up reading Jack London and spent his summers constructing working models of birch-bark canoes.

"Got enough duct tape?" I asked, looking around at the willows and alders mantling the banks of the river.

"Plenty," he said. "But we can't cut any live trees," he cautioned. "We're in a national park, remember."

"Right," I said. "I forgot."

"We'll use the stuff swept into the water, or rooted in dislodged chunks of undercut bank if we have to."

"Should be plenty. Think we should jury-rig just one canoe, fore and aft, or split up the parts?"

"Split 'em up, don't you think? Use the metal in the bows of both boats and bent willows in the stern."

"Should work."

It did work. In fact, we even came up with two different designs—based upon a refinement of the attachment point assembly and a resort, on the second effort, to bundling multiple slender shoots.

We even joked about filing a patent.

You can fix almost anything with duct tape. Heck, half of Alaska is held together with the stuff. And willows, whose supple strength has made them a construction staple among wilderness handymen since the dawn of the opposable thumb, can be contoured into anything short of a right angle.

I've got to admit that Bob and I were pretty proud of our effort (and Lisa and Linda not unduly impressed). It wasn't until both canoes were fully assembled, lab-tested, and approved, and Bob reached into the bag to remove the canoe's rolled-up floor mat, that the futility of our effort became apparent.

"Oh, no!" Bob exclaimed. "Look!"

There, lying on the ground at Bob's feet, were the missing parts. They hadn't been misplaced, just mispacked, hidden between the floor mat and walls of the container.

"We could just go with the canoes the way they are," I suggested. "I'll bet they'd do just fine."

"I'll bet they would, too," Bob said, locking eyes with me.

It was almost dinnertime by the time we got the boats disassembled and put back together again using stock, not substitute parts. Not that it mattered. We'd figured on a two-day layover anyway.

Hell of a waste of good duct tape, though.

Day 4

We woke late, again, but this time to clear skies, temperatures cold enough for jackets, and the sound of migrant birds overhead. The John is not only a corridor for creatures that go on two and four legs. It's also a verdant and welcoming avenue for Arctic birds whose first challenge, in their journey south, is to find passage across the Brooks. There were white-crowned sparrows and dark-eyed juncos in camp. American robins and lots and lots of yellow-rumped warblers in the willows.

We had a cold breakfast to help facilitate our start. Even so, we didn't launch until 12:30. Bob and Lisa leading, Linda and I happy to let them choose the water.

One of the reasons this stretch of Arctic river was selected was that it is easy. Fast enough to make time, forgiving enough to allow eyes to feast on scenery and not dangers ahead.

We've faced our white-water challenges, we four. Bested and been bested by rivers. Dried our sodden gear; patched our boats, loaded and lashed up, then done the next stretch. None of us, at this point in our lives, has much to prove or inclination to prove it, and wet gear is a bother, not a badge of honor.

We traveled about seven miles that first day on the water and put in on a cobble-strewn beach on the west bank that turned out to be a large island. Under a cloudless sky and the sass of gray jays, we pitched our golden-domed tents among summer green willows, just above the capricious reach of rivers that sometimes swell in the night.

Dinner conversation, over steaming bowls of jambalaya, was about the country we'd passed and birds we'd seen; whether butter or cream cheese was better on cinnamon and raisin or poppy seed bagels; and the fact that all of us wanted to be woken up in the night if anyone, attending a call to nature, saw northern lights.

Electronic dog fences and financial transfers were no longer thoughts, much less concerns. What was happening to travelers in the L.A. airport or how many innocents were being killed by car bombs in Iraq or what food item was being recalled for possible contamination or who, according to the tabloids, was sleeping with whom was divorcing whom was putting on weight or taking it off using what fad diet had no bearing.

All of us were completely under the spell of wilderness. It had drawn the dimensions of the universe down to here and compressed time to now. It had wiped our slates clean.

"We traveling tomorrow or laying over?" I asked, over my second piece of chocolate truffle cake.

"Lisa and I were talking about that," said Bob, who was collapsed into a Therm-a-Rest lounge chair and about as relaxed as a human being can be and still produce a pulse. "I know we planned for a ten-day trip, but if you guys like, we can stretch it to twelve. The weather's fine. It looks like great hiking country up above, and since we're heading for Bettles, we won't have to reschedule a pickup. There's a wedding we have to attend, but we can still add a couple of days to the trip if you guys are agreeable? So . . . layover here if you like."

You couldn't find two more agreeable people anywhere on the banks of the John.

We turned in under clear, windless skies and the sound of the river in our ears.

"Did you see the size of those bear tracks in the sand where we washed the dishes?" I whispered to Linda shortly after my head hit the pillow. But I wasn't quick enough. She was already asleep, the even sound of her breathing synchronized with the lap of the river against the shore.

There are few places a person can stand and look south onto Baffin Island, but this is one of them. The vantage point is our birding tour base camp on Bylot Island. The occasion is the Summer Solstice — practically speaking, the first day of autumn 2007.

ABOVE: *In the Arctic, if you are a lemming, a snow bunting, or a photographer, it pays to keep an eye to the sky. This adult parasitic jaeger on Bylot Island flew in to check out the human intruders. With the local lemming population depressed, jaegers and other hunters could look forward to a challenging breeding season.*

LEFT: *Fifty-five-gallon drums— the "state flower of Alaska." Expensive to fly out, discarded fuel drums flourish everywhere our species travels in the Arctic. Here, at an abandoned DEW Line site, they have been recycled to mark the approach to the still-active runway.*

RIGHT: *As our planet warms, the Arctic icecap melts. Here, our friend Bob Dittrick regards a bit of icecap in transition at the edge of the Beaufort Sea.*

BELOW: *Teshekpuk caribou migrating across blown-out coastal tundra. Saltwater intrusion sparked by global warming has altered the tundra environment here, and elsewhere, along this low and vulnerable coast.*

ABOVE: *That's melting permafrost and receding coastline on the left, Bob Dittrick on the right. According to Bob's GPS, we were paddling half a mile inland. Clearly there has been considerable coastal erosion along the Beaufort since those coordinates were plotted.*

BELOW: *In July, the Arctic is one big avian treasure trove. This red-throated loon, decked out in its maroon-throated finery, is a common breeder on small freshwater lakes.*

RIGHT: *This breeding semipalmated sandpiper might be king of the hill, but its reign is short. The breeding season over by July, this bird will soon be on its way to its winter retreat in South America.*

BELOW: *The perennial question in the Arctic is "Where are the caribou?" And the answer carries the weight of life and death. One bull, at least in a season past, was here.*

ABOVE: *The tundra is a living tapestry. Death is the transmutation of life, not the end. This caribou bone, which once supported an arctic deer, now supports a garden of lichen.*

BELOW: *Wherever the paths of humans and grizzly bears cross, bears have the right of way. Walk mindfully and respectfully and . . . it doesn't hurt to carry a can of Ursus-calibrated pepper spray.*

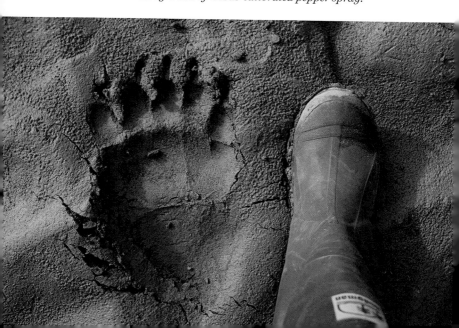

ABOVE: *It's looking like pancakes for breakfast tomorrow. Picking berries is a rite of autumn in the Arctic. On our August paddle down the John River, the flanking tundra was absolutely carpeted with blueberries and cranberries. Here, framed by Lisa Moorehead's feet, are the fruits of her labors.*

BELOW: *Yellow-tinged poplars, ice on the canoes, morning mist over the John River. Whew! Anybody feeling a bit of autumn chill around here?*

ABOVE: *Despite its scenic splendor, the John River, flowing south out of Brooks Range, is one of the Arctic's least-visited rivers. On our twelve-day trip, we encountered precisely three visitors.*

LEFT: *Gear on shore and float plane off. There goes our umbilical cord to the outside world. Let the fun begin!*

OPPOSITE: *Bob Dittrick and Lisa Moorehead of Wilderness Birding Adventures are advocates and practitioners of zero-impact wilderness travel. However, works of art, left in the hands of the universe, are excepted.*

ABOVE: *If you are lucky you may in the course of your life experience a* perfect moment—*a time and place where all the forces of the universe conspire to harmony. Here's one, now. Key elements include earth, water, sky, and Lisa.*

OPPOSITE: *Fireweed is Alaska's autumnal yardstick. When opening blossoms reach the spiky top, summer is nearly over. When fireweed goes to seed, as this one plainly has, it's irrefutably autumn.*

OPPOSITE: *In September, turning bearberry leaves paint St. Lawrence Island red. Don't look now, but winter's closing in.*

ABOVE: *Trappers Heimo and Edna Korth's cabin. It's snug and warm, and while some might balk at the idea of spending five Arctic winter months in a 14 by 14 foot cabin, you should know that the Korths spend little time at home. Seven days a week, in near and total darkness, the hardy couple are out checking their trap lines by snow machines.*

RIGHT: *On our last morning at Heimo's cabin, the thermometer read 14 degrees Fahrenheit. Just about right for the Arctic interior in early October. Balmy when you consider that in a few weeks, the daily high may reach only negative forty degrees.*

ABOVE: *Caught between a rock and a frozen place. This Churchill-based polar bear seems nonplussed by all the attention he's getting.*

BELOW: *A photo expedition to Churchill, Manitoba, the "Polar Bear Capital of the World," is every nature photographer's dream. Recognize Linda? She's the sixth lens down on the left.*

ABOVE: *A mother polar bear and her cubs come in to check out the new neighbors. Scenes like this are getting harder to find. Mortality among young bears is increasing because the melting icecap is reducing hunting success and forcing bears to swim greater distances across open seas.*

BELOW: *The famed Tundra Buggy Lodge. A home on wheels located right where polar bears gather to await the return of the winter ice sheet.*

A young male polar bear stranded on shore; open water beyond. It's a picture that says a thousand words, few of them encouraging for an animal whose survival is tied to the planet's most threatened habitat — the Arctic ice.

Day 5

She was saying goodbye in the old apartment. She was older, as old as the photo taken on her fiftieth birthday that she'd sent, but I was still driving the white '72 VW bug I bought, new, just before we got together. I could see it parked beneath the maple from the second-floor window of the room we lived in, in the bungalow colony that had, even now, already burned to the ground. I told her it would. She said she expected it.

Then we were with the guy she later married. We planned to drive through a tunnel, in the trees, but it had changed owners. Then it wasn't a tunnel anymore but an underground shopping district—like the streets and shops in the Old City of Jerusalem.

We walked from there. Forgot the car, it seemed. I considered chastising them for not reminding me about the car but decided not to. We walked on. Came upon a bunch of deer grazing on an abandoned railroad bed. Three young bucks, still in velvet. They raised their heads and looked at us. The look was fearless and appraising.

I woke and realized that the side of my face was wet.

Linda, on her side now, was still keeping time with the river. It was full light outside the tent.

I slipped out of my sleeping bag, remembering that, during the night, it had gotten cold enough to zip it up to the hood. Finding my boots, donning my jacket, I unzipped the door as quietly as a husband trying not to wake his sleeping wife can unzip a nylon zipper, then headed over to the cook tent to make coffee.

There is nothing in the world quite as good as cradling a mug of coffee in your hands on a cold morning, on a wilderness gravel bar. Just as there is nothing quite like sleeping in a tent, beside a neutral river, for unlocking dreams.

I've noticed this phenomenon before—anticipate it, in fact, am eager for it now, whenever I do a wilderness trip. The depths-plumbing, memory-cleansing dreams that stir from wherever memories hide once the noise of everyday life subsides and wilderness creeps in to pick the lock on your psyche.

When I was a child, I knew dreams as real as life. Even now, I still remember dreams I had when I was four and five years old. It's not memory. They are just there.

But the dreams I dream now, adult dreams sandwiched between adult days, are furtive and superficial. They evaporate when I wake and evade my best efforts to recall them.

Only in the wilderness do my dreams take on their former corporeal glory. Only here, when my mind is freed from niggling concerns, can I once again get down to the serious business of dreaming about matters worth dreaming about.

"But where the hell did that one come from?" I said to the mug, smiling ruefully. "Probably be a good idea not to mention it to Linda," I concluded. "Bet she'd like a cup of coffee though."

The only thing better than savoring a cup of coffee beside a mist-shrouded wilderness river is being snug in a sleeping bag, on a chilly morning, and having someone bring you a mug just the way you like it.

That may be even better than being lost in dreams.

After breakfast, we went hiking and berry picking. Lisa and Bob went one way, Linda and I another. We didn't plan it that way. It just happened that way.

I said we were hiking, but more accurately we went grazing. Our ambition was to hike up to the top of a nearby mountain, maybe a two-hour climb. But once we got above the tussock grass marsh, everywhere we turned there were blueberries begging to be eaten.

Big, fat, subtly sweet fruits that hung four and five and six to a cluster. I found one branch that boasted thirty-one berries along its four-inch length.

If grizzly bears dream, they dream of berries like these.

Berry picking is almost a national pastime in the Arctic. A rite of autumn. The locations of prime patches close to population centers are secrets shared only with the closest of friends. The long days of late summer find family groups of Native Americans and Anglo residents alike stooped, crouched, or sitting, filling cans and Tupperware canisters with the season's tribute.

We gorged ourselves. Tossed berries into each other's open mouths. Stained the seats and knees of our pants in indelible blue and laughed about it.

Halfway up the slope, Linda spotted something brown moving just over the crest of a hill. Instinctively, I looked down to make sure my can of bear spray hadn't come dislodged from its holster, then looked up to see antlers rise into the sky.

Caribou. Several, it turned out. All bulls. Fantastic.

Linda did a stalk, armed with her 200–400 zoom. Got close enough for a few quick shots, but when she tried to move in for a better angle, she jumped a bull bedded down in a ravine. Of course he spooked the other animals, who went hightailing—make that highantlering—off (spooked caribou always run with their heads held theatrically high).

Bob and Lisa beat us back to camp—with blueberry-stained hands and stories of their own. But when it comes to enjoying a wilderness experience, being first has about as much significance as time.

Day 6

It started like an ordinary day—if there is any such thing in the Arctic. Woke early to lightening skies, mountain peaks being strummed by fingers of clouds, and a fresh tribute of migrating songbirds in the willows.

There was mist on the river. Our island was glazed with dew.

It seemed, almost, that the rules partitioning earth and water had lapsed in the night. It looked, on this otherwise ordinary morning in the Arctic, like a world fresh out of the womb, on the eve of drawing breath.

Linda was still sleeping; Bob and Lisa, too. I went down for water, noting that the river had come up during the night, thinking that we'd been wise to carry the canoes up on the bank.

Coffee in hand, I decided to take a tour of the island, which took less time than I'd hoped. The island was small, a mile around at most. If not for the multitude of migrating (and resident) birds that begged watching and the tracks of bear and moose and wolf and beaver and mink that needed study, the walk would have been even shorter. By the time I completed my circuit, the sun was just peeking over a saddle in the ridge. The mountains west of the river were fully illuminated, those to the east still in eclipse. The river was the dividing point, partitioning the world into sunlight and shadow.

The camp was still quiet. I poured another mug of coffee and walked down to be close to the sound of the river and find a spot to scan for birds. A grounded log proved ideal. Uprooted by spring floods. Scoured and polished by ice down to gray wood. It waited, patiently, for the next upheaval to move it along or time to wear it down. But it was going nowhere today, and it made a dry and comfortable seat.

First mugs of coffee are for waking. Second mugs are for savoring, and my highest ambition was to savor the hell out of this one. It wasn't until I brought the mug to my mouth, inhaling the richness and feeling the warmth flood my mouth, that I spied Lisa.

She was down the beach, half cloaked in river mist. She was kneeling and building a pyramid of river-turned stones atop the curve of a river-polished log, bent like a rainbow. Half her sculpture was stone. Half was air. Two elements so antagonistic to union that they make water and oil seem soluble.

She was, or seemed, oblivious to my presence and absorbed in her project. A mature woman, with long hair, pixie features, and an expression like a child trying to look serious. She is, among her many other accomplishments, an admirer and self-proclaimed apprentice of the English sculptor Andy Goldsworthy, whose ephemeral art fuses man and nature and who enlists, as his artistic partner, the capricious indulgence of time.

He sculpts with ice. He sculpts with branches. He sculpts, as Lisa was doing, with stone. Neither the master nor his student uses any material not found in nature. The mortar that held Lisa's structure together was an amalgam of friction and gravity. But the miracle of combination sprouting from her fingers came from within. If you asked me to pin a name to this secret ingredient, I'd call it "harmony." If you asked me why the universe suffered her effort, why it didn't impose its iron laws of gravity, I'd say it was because an ever-changing universe must yearn for balance, too. In Lisa, on this beach, on this morning, the universe recognized a confederate and ally.

I took another sip of coffee. Sipped because it was still hot, and the air was chill, and on this beach, at this moment, the balance was perfect. Lisa, who was nearing the delicate end of her project, had risen to search for a last few, most critical of stones. So intent was she that the northern goshawk that crossed the river taking a perch atop a tall, dead spruce went unnoticed. A beautiful bird, the color of river mist, that took in the scene below, conscious of all of it but indifferent to most.

That's when I realized I was living a *perfect moment.* A time and place when all the forces of the universe conspire to utter harmony. You don't second-guess a perfect moment any more than you can create one. Like magic, like the infinitely improbable juxtaposition of energy and matter that occurs every moment of every day, perfect moments just happen.

The trick is recognizing them.

This was the third in my life. But my very first *perfect moment*—when harmony and awareness became one—was many years ago.

I was ten, maybe eleven. It was summer. Near midmorning, because while the sunlight pouring through the picture window was warm, the interior of our home still lingered under the spell of night-cooled air.

I was sitting in my father's chair. Wholly absorbed in Sheila Burnford's story about an animal trio who cross a wilderness in order to be reunited with their human family. The book was called *The Incredible Journey.*

In the kitchen my mother was making the small, comforting noises of her daily routine. The AM radio was playing the elegiac strains of the summer's runaway hit song, "Cast Your Fate to the Wind." In the back of my mind lay the delicious understanding that I would go outside, soon. Maybe go down to "the ponds." Fish, or skip stones. But not yet. Not until I decided. Because it was so comfortable. Here. Now. And because the story in my hands was so wonderful.

Then the song reached the part, near the end, when the piano's notes pause, and the sound of the last note fades into a silence that lingers. And you hold your breath, waiting for the composition's final enchantment, when, from that silence, the piano awakens again.

It was in the silence of that pause that I realized that what I was living was a *perfect moment*. Realized that all the forces and elements of the universe had been brought into focus and balance, and that, in the pregnant pause, the universe was inviting my awareness.

It occurred to me that I should commit every detail to memory. Because I'd lived long enough by then to know, or at least suspect, that *perfect moments* are not every day and that having a *perfect moment* logged in memory could prove very useful—at the very least a point of reference against which to measure all the moments of a human life that fall short.

It's been many years since that morning. I have, to my great fortune, come to learn that, while *perfect moments* are not singular, they are, just as I suspected, rare. They seem never alike, no more than any moment in time is like another, but they are special. Worth a memory at least.

Lisa completed her search, then the sculpture. As I watched, she stood, bestowing upon it a creator's joy. Absorbing from it the gift of its being.

Just like that morning years ago, I brought my mind to bear and committed to memory all the details of the moment.

Warm light to the west and cool shadow to the east. The

comforting sound of the river, the clean smell of autumn in the air, the warmed smoothness of the log beneath me, a watching hawk above, and a woman—a friend—standing on a beach paved in river-turned stone, communing with the sculpture that she and the universe had created and that would last as long as it was suffered to be.

Which in this case outlasted the *perfect moment* because, abruptly, Lisa turned and started down the beach to go into her yoga routine, flushing the goshawk, which disappeared into the trees, capping the moment.

For breakfast, we had blueberry pancakes that were more berry than batter and the fruits of yesterday's gathering.

Then we broke camp. Loaded the canoes. Policed the area, making sure we were leaving it as we'd found it. Except for Lisa's sculpture.

We left that in the hands of the universe. It was still there last time I looked.

Day 7

We spent the night on the east side of the river, just below Wolverine Creek—about a ten-mile paddle from Goldsworthy Beach (as I named the place). When we arrived, we were distressed to see the fire remains from previous campers and a number of large rocks dislodged. It's a small matter, arguably, insofar as all traces of the summer season's activity would be erased by winter ice and spring flood. But nobody who prizes a wilderness experience deserves to suffer someone else's discourtesy, and nobody who values wilderness should ever leave a campsite in a state less pristine than they found it.

Works of art, left in the hands of the universe, excepting.

It was colder this morning. First morning that gloves went

on with jackets. While we were eating our breakfast of oatmeal and blueberries, Linda suddenly asked to borrow binoculars.

"Bears on the ridge," she announced, handing the binoculars back.

Sure enough, just across the river, a female black bear and her cub were eating their way across the landscape. Further scanning, along ridgetops that were tinged with autumn red, turned up another larger, probably male black bear about two miles upriver doing much the same thing. Gorging himself on berries. Bulking up the layer of fat that would see him through an Arctic winter.

"Surprised we haven't seen any before," Bob observed. "There're tracks everywhere."

There were, too. Black bear and griz. In fact, the island we were on, near the mouths of two sizable valleys—one on the east side of the river, and the one bearing Wolverine Creek on the west—was, for obvious reasons, a major steppingstone for animals moving east and west.

Not for this reason, we broke camp and continued on. Bob and I were looking forward to catching some grayling, and the John is, for the most part, too turbid to be suitable for these small, beautiful Arctic Salmonidae. Because they are slow-growing in Arctic waters, a twelve-inch grayling is a keeper, fourteen inches confers bragging rights, and a fifteen-inch grayling constitutes a trophy.

What we needed was a clear, grayling-friendly feeder stream, and several streams downriver seemed promising.

We were hardly a mile from camp when Linda spotted something on the bluff above the river and directed my attention to it by saying, loudly, *"Ohmygodwolf!"*

Forgetting the two-way radio in my pocket, I relayed Linda's message to Bob and Lisa, who were ahead, by employing the ancient art of shouting. As methods of transmitting information go, shouting is very effective at moderately long range, but it has its shortcomings.

For instance, and in this case, it prompted the wolf, a white one, to disappear (although our energetic arm waving and pointing might also have influenced its decision to make itself scarce). Bob and Lisa never got a look at the animal and over lunch took time to counsel us on the considerable advantages inherent in the use of two-way radios.

What are friends for?

Day 8

A beautiful day on the river, but still and hot! Temperatures in the eighties, which is not at all uncommon for the interior of Alaska in midsummer (cooked, as it is, under nonstop sunlight), but it was certainly unusual now! We paddled about fifteen river miles, through country so magnificent it left an ache when you were forced to look away (to avoid a submerged log or a "sweeper" projecting from the bank).

The summer had been a wet one (in fact, earlier groups had been pinned down by high waters). Flood damage was evident all along the banks. While the John is an easy paddle, the flooding had dislodged a lot of trees and cut a few new channels, promising that inattentiveness on the part of canoeists would not go unpunished.

Of course you simply cannot help but admire the mountains (despite the risks). The southern Brooks are a fascinating mix. Sometimes as stark and barren as the Mojave range. In places as majestic, sculpted, and tree-covered as the Canadian Rockies. At times intimate; at times forbidding.

Intimate, because they come right down to the banks of the river. You can paddle over to them. You can touch them. Forbidding because the craggy, sedimentary crust seems sharp enough to cut the bellies of clouds, and the many nooks and crannies host eye-defeating shadows that hide only your imagination knows what.

Here and there are touches of colors; pastel shades of pinks that run across hillsides like fresh scars. But for the most part, the Brooks are a stark, indifferent gray. If you've ever driven through northeastern Pennsylvania and seen the piles of shale vomited up by the coal-mining industry, you have been offered a glimpse of the Brooks.

The river, by comparison, seems like an avenue of peace flowing through an angry landscape. Unless, as a result of incaution, you get sucked into the bank by the current or slammed by a sweeper—the price you pay for admiring the scenery around you.

We decided to camp at a place that offered a superb view of the aptly named Gunsight Mountain—a gray mass of stone notched like the rear sight on a rifle. Lentils for dinner. Layover tomorrow. This could be the most picturesque stop on the trip (but it's a tight field).

DAY 9

Woke early (as usual) to clear skies that darkened quickly with clouds racing south. No bugs. No animal sounds except for the clucking of robins and the chatter of red squirrels. Pretty cold. Mid-thirties I'd guess. First two-jacket morning. By the time the rest of the crew rose for a breakfast of blueberries held together with oatmeal, the clouds were gone, temperatures rising quickly. Linda and I decided to go for a hike that started badly. Turned out we were on another island, and the first four hundred yards meant bushwhacking through alders that took us north of where we wanted to go.

If you've ever bushwhacked through alders, you know exactly what I'm talking about. If you haven't, count your blessings.

We were gone for the balance of the day (detained, once again and at every other step, by a carpet of blueberries), and by the time we got back, Bob and Lisa were gone. Linda and I took advantage of the seclusion and moderate temperatures to have a refreshing (and overdue) bath. The water wasn't ice cold, but it was cold enough that we didn't dawdle. Cold enough to give you an "ice-cream headache" when you dunked to get the soap out of your hair.

Biodegradable soap, of course.

Dunk, wet down. Scream! Soap up. Dunk, rinse. Scream! Dry hurriedly and slip into clean clothes.

Shortly after we dressed, we looked up to see a young man in a one-man paddler's raft go bobbing by. Except for occasional bush planes, he was the only person we'd seen on the trip. We waved, he waved, then passed on.

It was nice to see a young person out enjoying the wilderness. Chances were, he was thinking it was nice to see two old people enjoying the wilderness.

There is nothing incompatible in these thoughts.

During the soaping-up process, I thought I saw fish rise in the still waters of an oxbow. Going back later, I hooked and lost two northern pike and landed a third using light tackle and a small spoon. Got back to camp in time to have the still-wiggling fish added to the chowder Bob was making. From river to gullet, I'd guess the elapsed time for Mr. Pike was less than thirty minutes.

Fish hardly gets fresher than that.

Day 10

We woke to an odd clucking just outside the tent.

"Recognize that?" Linda asked.

"No," I said. "Not even sure it's a bird."

The source of the sound proved to be a spruce grouse, who it seemed, was perplexed by the gold-domed tent in its path. Not known for its intellect, in fact, known throughout the north country as the "fool hen," the bird fussed about for a few minutes and was saved from Linda's photographic proclivities only by the early hour and poor light.

Long travel day, today. The weather's been spectacular (no rain since the day we landed), but we'd been dawdling and didn't want to have to make up miles if the weather turned gnarly and we got pinned down for a day. The current was slowing as the mountains grew tamer. According to the muscles in my arms and shoulders, the twenty-five river miles we logged today were every bit of twenty-five miles.

We camped on the east shore, on another large island that was rimmed with tracks and paved with river-sculpted stones. It seems the farther we travel the more varied and attractive the stones on the beach become. I fished for a bit with no luck. Bob set a line for burbot, also no luck. Pesto for dinner tonight and another travel day tomorrow.

Day 11

Another cold morning. Cloudy, too. The surrounding mountains have grown curvaceous, lost their edge, and the color on the higher hilltops is autumn red. Bear mush (hot cereal) for breakfast and then another long paddle day.

We didn't travel as far as planned, but the day's paddle still carried us out of the Brooks. The river was framed now by birches and poplars, which seemed to be turning yellow by the minute. The current was slow and in places almost non-existent. I think, too, all of us were still tired from the day before.

Birds—migrants, anyway—were noticeably absent. But American three-toed woodpeckers, year-round residents, were suddenly everywhere.

The clouds broke by three, and the day warmed up. We put in early, on a beach that shows on the topo maps as pretty significant. Significant and used. Once again we were faced with someone else's lack of etiquette. But good beaches get scarcer in the southern reaches of the river, and we decided to just suck it up and settle.

The view was expansive, and this proved to be important, because just after midnight we were awakened by the crunch of Bob's shoes on gravel and the eagerly anticipated announcement.

"Hey, guys. The aurora is showing."

Nothing, short of shouting "bear in camp," could have gotten us out of our bags quicker, and in short order (in about as much time as it takes for two people, in a small tent, to fight their way past sleeping bag zippers that always jam when you are in a hurry and fit the right [and left] shoes to the right [and left] feet) we joined Bob and Lisa by the river to take in the show.

The aurora borealis, also called the "northern lights," are not limited to the Arctic; in fact, they are not even limited to the Northern Hemisphere, as the name suggests. The root of *borealis* is Boreas, the name of the Greek god of the north wind. The first place I ever witnessed the celebrated upper atmosphere light show was in Kansas, and while not common, auroras are annual to semiannual in our home state of New Jersey.

But it is in the north, in an area known as the auroral zone, that the most spectacular displays are most often viewed—on average between 200 and 250 nights per year. This zone is located between 60 and 70 degrees north latitude. The John lies at 67 degrees—so it's ground zero for northern lights watchers. The lights themselves are the products of electrons emanating from the sun, ferried to earth by solar winds, that strike gas molecules (principally oxygen) in the earth's upper atmosphere, "exciting" them to glow. It is the same lighting principle harnessed in a neon light, but of course, the energy output is considerably greater in space.

This energetic interplay between the sun and the earth's gaseous outer layer occurs in the ionosphere, between 60 and 160 miles above the earth's surface. It is concentrated around our two magnetic poles, creating what amounts to a high-altitude, incandescent, oval light bulb that in the Northern Hemisphere overlies northern Europe, Greenland, the United States, and Asia.

While the oval is fixed around the magnetic pole, it is not static. It expands and shrinks in response to the energy output of the sun. When sun activity is subdued, the "auroral oval" shrinks, drawing north of 70 degrees north latitude, and is visible only in more northern regions. When the sun's activity intensifies, bombarding the earth with large amounts of energy, the oval expands, extending at times as far south as 50 degrees (about the latitude of London). At such times, the aurora can be viewed much farther south than normal.

The most common form the aurora takes is greenish white curtains—the product of oxygen atoms being "excited" in the middle altitudes of the aurora belt. Dark red auroras also involve oxygen but are forged at higher altitudes, in the near-perfect vacuum of space. The bright red or rose trim sometimes seen on the hems of the green curtains is created at lower altitudes and involves the excitation of nitrogen atoms.

Most of our understanding of the aurora was forged during the twentieth century. But fascination with the dancing lights goes back much further in human history. Aristotle likened the aurora to glowing air and suggested that the source was "chasms" in the sky. And in medieval times, in Italy and France, appearances of blood-red auroras were feared as augurs of impending war.

Many Native, northern cultures, including the Inuit, believe the lights are the spirits of the dead, engaged in a spirited ball game—one that involves the skull of a dead walrus and whose objective is to plant the skull, tusks down, in the celestial snowfields upon which the game is played. In fact, the name for the aurora in the Yupik tongue is *aqsarniit,* which means "football players."

The Inuit also ascribe sound to the lights, a hissing or whistle, and even reactive properties. By whistling, the Inuit believe, it is possible to draw the spirit lights near, sometimes frighteningly close. Eskimo children are cautioned to be respectful and discreet.

And before you think to chastise aboriginal people's superstitions, you should know that a whole tourist industry has blossomed in Fairbanks and Yellowknife focused upon satisfying the conjugal aspirations of newlywed Japanese couples. In Japanese culture, to conceive a child beneath the northern lights is considered good luck.

From our vantage, both physical and cultural, there was nothing to fear from the light show going on north and east of the John, as that portion of the planet we were on slid beneath a modestly "excited" auroral oval.

Our enthusiasm levels were quite elevated. Elevated by the shimmering beauty of one of the planet's most spectacular natural events. Enhanced by the factor of friendship. Succored by our surroundings and our entitling detachment.

Given poignancy by the understanding that our journey was drawing to an end. In just two days' time (since it was now past midnight), the curtain would fall. We would have to return to the world as we'd left it.

We stayed until the lights were nearly overhead. Shimmering phantoms, ignited by the sun but brought to life by our eyes, they spread like luminous dye in ink-dark water, then evaporated like mist in sunlight. I don't know how long we watched. An hour, certainly, maybe more. In the end, with smiles and second "good nights," the four of us surrendered to our nagging need for sleep and whatever dreams the aurora might have kindled.

In the morning the island was touched with frost, our overturned canoes and the flies of the tents sheathed in ice. The curtain had fallen on summer, too.

DAY 12

The last paddle day. Despite the evening interruption, we were all up early. Combating the chill in the air with mugs of coffee and steaming bowls of bear mush. Listening to the late-season medley of sound. The mewing of gray jays. The half songs of fox sparrows. The brittle chips of juncos. The raspy admonishments of boreal chickadees. The bleat of a Swainson's thrush.

It's funny, but I'd been hearing these bird sounds nearly every morning. Only now, with the trip drawing to its close, did I find myself hanging on every note.

The paddle was long but leisurely. The day pleasant but hot. In its lower reaches, the John wanders quite a bit, turning north before meandering south to meet up with the Koyukuk. There were beaver workings everywhere, attesting to a sizable population and the industrious nature of this large rodent (not to mention the imminence of winter). With snow on the ground, and the river locked in ice, the food these bark-gnawing fur bearers use to see them through the winter comes from the branches they collect and cache on the river bottom. The time for stockpiling was now.

We traveled about fifteen miles and beached several hundred yards above the confluence. Made camp. Took advantage of the warm temperatures to lather up in the river. And then . . .

"I'm going for a walk," I said to the relaxed and semiprone form of Linda, who was on the beach next to Lisa. Both were reading.

"How far?" she asked, not looking up.

"Dunno," I said.

"How long?"

"Can't say. Couple hours I'd guess."

Lisa, who, likewise, had not looked up, closed her book. Closed her eyes. Leaned back and let the strength of the autumn sun shine full in her face, savoring the molten glow of it on her eyelids.

We were, all of us, in our own ways, preparing ourselves for the end. Maneuvering for distance. Redirecting our minds to the engagement of issues and matters and tasks and obligations that our time on the river had put on hold.

"Okay," she said. "See you later." It was the answer I expected and, in fact, wanted. Fact was, I was feeling the need for distance, too.

I walked south to the Koyukuk, then east, hugging the shore when I could, climbing the bank and navigating game trails where floodwaters had erased the bank. There were fewer tracks, fewer animals. Only four air miles from Bettles, this was to be expected. Still, you can run into moose just about anywhere, and the supersize pile of reconstituted blueberry plopped in the middle of a game trail assured me that there was at least one large bear in the neighborhood and that his appetite was fine.

The one thing in superabundance was river-turned stones. While every place we'd camped might have served as a quarry, the banks of the Koyukuk were the mother lode.

I'm not a practicing rock hound. In fact, and as related in one of the predecessors to this book, *Bayshore Summer,* I harbor a vestigial grudge against geology. A childhood spent digging and hauling the rocks the Laurentide ice sheet dumped in our suburban yard ensured that I would never own a home with a rock garden.

Yet and still, I've always had a honed appreciation for stones worked by water—particularly the flat, smooth, perfectly round and aerodynamic kind. Stones whose obvious purpose is to be encircled by a thumb and an index finger and danced across the surface of a lake or pond or river.

And I have always been attracted to things of beauty. When I was a child, my pockets were collecting sacks for the treasures found during the day. Bird feathers, well-patterned acorns, praying mantis egg cases, snakeskins, and of course, and maybe especially, beautiful stones.

On my walk along the banks of the Koyukuk, I realized that I was in a skipper finder's heaven. Everywhere I turned, there were stones that begged hands to enfold them and pockets to encase them.

Bending down, I picked up one that was shaped like a gray dome of sky with an encircling crown of quartz.

It's like the auroral oval, I thought. Clearly meant to be a keepsake. So I dropped it in my pocket.

I found another kidney-shaped beauty, black as night and enlivened by stars, that fit my hand like it was custom-made (and it found its way into my pocket, too).

Then another that was perfect, I mean perfectly round (except for one small flat area designed to keep the marvel from rolling away on your desk) and another that was so obviously phallic it was beyond circumspect, and another marvelously marbled white-on-gray one that was shaped like a trickling tear.

Both jacket pockets were full, but then I got into a stretch where beautifully colored stones simply paved the banks. River-polished gems the color of arterial blood and smooth green marvels that seemed like frozen drops of Arctic seas.

I was out of storage space now. No room in pockets or hands. I chided myself for not bringing a daypack, and then I found a stone that I absolutely could not live without. It was shaped like a perfect heart and had, embedded in its perfectly smoothed face, a single raised garnet.

I have got to give this to Linda, I said, leaning over, losing the jade green beauty clutched in my hand and the teardrop that was squeezed from my pocket.

Now what?

Gathering all my prizes, I brought the collection to an open, sandy spot and laid them out for evaluation and culling, but none seemed less desirable than the others.

I considered going back to get a daypack but, looking at the angle of the sun, knew there would not be time—not today or tomorrow. The trip was over. And then I thought how uncomfortable the walk back was going to be with my pockets filled with rocks and then, maybe, how silly, too.

Walking back to camp across a landscape paved with perfect stones already burdened with stones collected along the way. It was certain I'd find more. But could I possibly find better stones than these?

I couldn't decide. I wonder if you could either. If you had the choice. If I gave you the choice, now.

The choice . . .

Of undoing all the choices you have already made in your life, in return for the latitude to make and live them all again. In the end, your pockets will be full. But the price is losing all you have now.

Would you do it?

Or . . . maybe this isn't fair. Force you to throw your whole life away like that. Tell you what I'm going to do. I'm going to make you an offer that's almost too good to refuse.

What if we don't start the game over? What if we extend this one? Let you scour fresh, new shores with a practiced eye and keep all you find plus, *plus* I'll let you keep one stone from your first run down the beach. The best of the best. Pick of the litter. You forfeit the rest.

Or, you can keep *all* the runners-up you found on your way down, *plus* all the ones you find from here on in, but you must give up that best one. I'll even throw in a free daypack.

The catch? There's little chance you'll ever find as good a stone as the one you left behind. The best. Or the rest. It's your life.

"How was your walk?" Linda asked later. "You were gone a long time."

"Fine."

"What's that in you hand?"

"Here," I said. "I've got something for you."

DAY 13, AUGUST 24

Well, that was about as much fun as this aging baby boomer can stand. We got up at 4:30 (yep, watch is back on). We needed to catch the 1:00 P.M. flight out of Bettles to Fairbanks, since Bob and Lisa were pressed to meet that wedding obligation.

I've lined canoes—i.e., towed canoes, upstream, against the current—before, but I'd never done it any appreciable distance, and I'd never done it in water as high and fast-moving as we experienced on the Koyukuk.

Fortunately, the weather was fine. The incredible luck we'd enjoyed throughout the trip held. We got off about 6:30, Bob and Lisa in the lead. Paddled across the mouth of the John and landed on the north bank of the Koyukuk. Then, with Linda holding the lead rope, me trailing, we began walking and wading along the river, towing the canoe along.

There are two important considerations when lining. First, don't get into water so fast and deep it fills your hip boots or sweeps you away. One is almost as bad as the other, and frankly, it's common for both to happen more or less simultaneously.

The other important thing is to mind your bow. Keep it straight and running parallel to the bank. Don't let it nose out into the current or the boat will turn sideways. Either you will lose your grip (and maybe the boat) or the boat will swamp. Neither prospect is appealing.

We had only one bad moment (not counting the several times the water crept up to near hip-boot-topping levels). Linda had the bow get away from her as we entered a particularly ugly set of rapids, and while she is really strong, she is also only 110 pounds.

"I can't hold the line," she shouted. "Help me."

A mere fifteen feet away, I doubted I could get there in time, and when the boat swamped, as it was plainly getting ready to do, it was doubtful that even the two of us could have prevented it from becoming a derelict, heading downstream.

"Let go," I shouted, and Linda did, letting the bow spin into the current as I braced myself, shortened the line, and leaned back to take the strain.

Luckily, the stern was still in fairly tranquil water, and the line was tight enough to keep the canoe from cartwheeling away.

It was over four miles to Bettles. We arrived a little after 11:00, still mostly dry, with two canoes and all our gear but just two hours to break down the boats, portage our stuff to the road, bum a ride out to the airfield, and catch the plane.

Which we did.

Three hours later we were standing outside Hot Licks in Fairbanks savoring four of the most generous and well-deserved ice-cream cones ever scooped and served. We'd originally planned to spend the night in Fairbanks, but our decision to extend the trip precluded this plan. Instead, we loaded up the truck and headed for Eagle River, pulling into the driveway just after 1:00 A.M.

The dogs were fine, overjoyed to see us. We went to bed near drunk with exhaustion.

I dreamed I had a plane to catch but couldn't remember where I was going or where I'd parked the car. Linda said it was on the other side of the river but needed a part. I couldn't understand why it was on the other side of the river or how it got there. There must have been a road, but it was gone now. I hated to see that car on the beach where it didn't belong and felt bad that I was going to be late. At least the car would be gone in the spring.

CHAPTER 6

Moon Month of Akullirut (August–September),
"Caribou Hair Thickens"

Men Without Buntings

St. Lawrence Island, Alaska

The morning started badly. Wind-driven rain on the bedroom window. A throat that felt like it had been worked over with a file. A coffeemaker that threw a tantrum all over the counter, then the kitchen floor. But at least I didn't have a hangover—one of the underappreciated benefits of being in the Native village of Gambell. By tribal ordinance, this residence of 660 Siberian Yupik people situated on the northwestern tip of St. Lawrence Island is dry. Spooning grounds out of the mug with two fingers, I walked across the living room, fell into one of the folding camp chairs, and helped myself to several handfuls of Goldfish crackers—passing on the pretzels, peanuts, and candy bar sampler that constituted the balance of the room's centerpiece snack display.

It seemed a little early for candy.

The womenfolk (including Linda) were gone. The "official" part of Wilderness Birding Adventures's Fall Gambell birding tour was over. But with the house under contract until mid-September, and migrant birds still coming through, it has become Bob Dittrick's habit to linger in Gambell and open the door to a band of Alaska-based birding friends.

Male friends. A gang of mostly aging baby boomers, united by their interest in birding and cemented by years of friendship, who spend a week or two or three together each year. Enjoying, for a short time, a life unfettered by interchromosomal compromise. Living the happy, carefree, and young-as-we-dream-ourselves-to-be lives that wives have always darkly suspected and discussed, at length, at health spas, the gym, or over lunch with "the girls."

Not that I was thinking about this as I slurped my coffee. Listening for signs of life from the second floor. Waiting for the caffeine to neutralize the sludge in my mind. Letting my thoughts move, in a lazy, laissez-faire fashion, across the room that was the combination meeting room, dining room, drying room, storage locker, library, computer lab, and snack counter.

About the size of a suburban bedroom, with tile flooring, tile ceiling, and wood panel walls, the construction is fairly typical of "old Gambell." Rustic, sturdy, lived in, and weathered—as only buildings built in the face of Bering Sea weather can weather.

The wealth of drying racks and hooks sprouting from the

walls and ceilings as well as the water-stained tiles attest to the inclement nature of that weather. So, too, do the double-door mudrooms on opposing sides of the house. Even on St. Lawrence Island, winds commonly come from one direction at a time.

The rest of the house consists of a small kitchen, two downstairs bedrooms, and a large attic turned flophouse. The single bathroom (and all the plumbing) is downstairs. This is why I was confident that the water stains on the ceiling tile were weather-related.

Furniture was spare, decorations few. A framed Picasso print, a laminated painting of the Last Supper. A bare fluorescent light that needed coaxing. The home's Native occupants were rooming with relatives in the village so that the enterprising owner could take advantage of Gambell's brief tourist season by converting the home into a temporary rental.

They—mom and the kids—came in now and again to get clothes or use the shower, but we rarely saw them, and I never had the opportunity to ask them how they regarded the transformation of their home into a birding operations center.

How puzzling, or amusing, it must have been to see their living room turned into a closet filled with drying outdoor gear, the floor sporting laptop computers at every outlet, enough optics to stock a New York camera store, and a table covered with books bearing such arcane titles as *Birds of the Seward Peninsula, Gulls of the Americas, Birds of the USSR, Birds of Thailand, Birds of Japan,* and two copies of *Birds of Korea* (not to mention multiple copies of the *National Geographic Field Guide to the Birds of North America*).

If this array of titles seems puzzling to you, it can only mean that you are not a serious birder and therefore do not realize St. Lawrence Island's strategic importance. Located a scant thirty-eight miles from eastern Siberia, it is nevertheless United States territory. In spring and fall, a smattering of migrating birds, hailing from Asia, overshoot the mainland, fly out across the waters of the Bering Sea, and set their tired wings down on Gambell, where they become, de facto, "countable" on a birder's North American life list. Yes, many far northern species are native to both Asia and North America, but a compelling number are not. In fact, many to most of the species illustrated in the books arrayed on the table do not breed and only rarely (if ever) occur, as vagrants, in North America.

So if you fall among the ranks of North American birders who have already seen most of the birds that your native continent has to offer, and you want to bulk up your life list with Asian waifs, then Gambell is the place for you. In fact, the tiny village has probably produced more first North American records than any municipality in North America.

Needless to say, my housemates fell into this narrow band of the human spectrum.

"This must be the only place this side of Seoul with two copies of *Birds of Korea*," I mused as I chewed the last mouthful of coffee, gave thought to going for a refill, and heard the measured tread of feet, moving carefully in the dark, finding their way downstairs.

The door opened to disclose the groggy but otherwise functioning form of Pat Pourchot, who mumbled a greeting and navigated a course toward the bathroom.

Sometimes, there are matters more pressing than coffee.

A former state senator, he enjoys a more than passing resemblance to Socrates and shares, with the learned philosopher, a keen and questioning mind.

Next to surrender to consciousness and gravity was Bob, whose measured thumps were identified by a slight arrhythmia—a token of multiple skiing accidents compounded by assorted misadventures involving bush planes, automobiles, and tumbles from high places.

"Morning," he acknowledged, ambling past. Noting the closed door to the bathroom. Heading for the kitchen instead. Filling a mug. Assessing the preponderance of roughage in the solution. Saying nothing.

"Sleep well?" I invited, after his six-foot, three-inch frame got settled in a chair.

"Kinda," he said. "Someone was sure sawin' logs down here," he said, not saying it was me.

"Must have been the rain," I offered.

"No, it was snoring," he said, treating me to a knowing smile before giving his attention to the coffee. "Course Sonneborn's reading habits make life interesting, too."

Dave Sonneborn, Dr. Dave Sonneborn, cardiovascular surgeon, lays claim to Alaska's top bird list, a total of four hundred species for the state. In addition to being Anchorage's go-to person when middle-aged hearts crap out, Dave is a voracious reader whose sleeping habits seem to have been permanently altered by the sleep-deprived residency all physicians must endure. At odd and not infrequent intervals during the night, second-floor tenants could count on the sight of the doctor reading under the glow of his headlamp.

Just then James Levison appeared, from around the corner, looking awake and trim. A retired administrator at University of Alaska, Fairbanks, and a somewhat recent convert to birding, he has the square-jawed look and no-nonsense bearing of a marine sergeant. Not the kind that kids meet at the booth at the county fair. The kind that greets recruits when they step off the bus at Parris Island.

With a nod in our direction, he advanced into the kitchen and started laying out breakfast just ahead of James Huntington, whose wiry frame moved quickly through the room and, with characteristic luck, managed to get to the door to the bathroom just as Pat was exiting, beating the crowd.

A mail carrier from Iowa City, he looks like a cross between Marty Feldman and Salvador Dalí and nurtures a passion for chasing birds that is exceeded only by his genial good nature. His life list on that morning in September stood at 847, putting James well up in the Double O class of North American birders—the Top Ten.

Aaron Lang was next, wearing his WBA cap and blinking in the light. Wilderness Birding Adventures's young ace, at thirty-one he was, by far, the youngest in the group. Looking somewhat like a tall, gaunt Arnold Schwarzenegger, Aaron has an uncanny ability to make himself liked by just about everybody he meets. Aiding him in this regard are a quick mind and a biting humor.

Eric Myers was suddenly among us. Intense, bespectacled, and hours-in-the-gym fit, Eric is an ardent conservationist who supports multiple good causes for a living.

Porter (Dave Porter), retired chief ranger with Denali State Park, stumbled down next. He mumbled something incoherent. Commandeered a strategic position between the kitchen and the bathroom. Waited.

Last to appear on the scene was the good Dr. Sonneborn, who stood in the middle of the room, looking like the figure of Moses in a black T-shirt and untied running shoes. Becoming mindful of an open chair, he plopped himself down, picked up a copy of *The New Yorker,* and started reading.

Everyone present and accounted for. Nine men, ranging in age from thirty-one to sixty-five (with a median age of fifty-eight), each in his own fashion waking to a new day, in a rented home in a Native village, while rain lashed at the windows and the outside world offered small hints that, once again, the earth would keep its 4.54-billion-year-old streak alive and treat inhabitants to a dawn.

"Anybody got a weather report?" Porter asked all of us.

Aaron, with the reflexes of a thirty-one-year-old, went for the telephone and dialed the NOAA number, while Bob reached for his newest electronic wiz-gadget that can give you anything from the pollen count to a measure of seismic activity. "Barometer's goin' up," he pronounced. Good news as far as it went. There hadn't been a lot of it during our time on the island.

West winds are what all Gambell birders pray for. The kind that sweep Siberian birds this way.

Every morning (every morning the weather falls short of life-threatening, anyway) Gambell's birders muster to conduct a sweep of the "Near" and "Far" Bone Yards. These wormwood-covered middens constitute the only game in town for birds seeking vegetative cover. Paul Lehman, a California birder who has made Gambell close to a second home, commonly orchestrates the sweeps. Having visited Gambell every autumn since 1992, he has not only earned the nickname "Mr. Gambell" but secured a place on the village council's "Happy Birthday" e-mail list.

But the days had been dominated by winds from the east and south, ferrying to the island birds such as American redstart and fox sparrow—birds that I could easily, and with a good deal less expense, have seen at home. Sweeps of the boneyards, thus far and for the most part, had failed to turn up the bounty of Asian waifs everyone dreamed of.

"Southwest winds this morning," Aaron relayed, pausing. "Going east, then south again tonight." Not the worst news, but not the best either. A little bit of west is better than no west at all.

"Muffin up," Sergeant James announced from the kitchen, but nobody rose to claim it.

Porter, his strategy and perseverance paying off, followed James in the bathroom.

"Good of you to join us, James," quipped Aaron, as the mail carrier moved into the room.

"I've been up for hours," he lied, which reminded him. "Bob, was it you who changed the time on my alarm and hid it under my clothes?"

"Why would I want to do that?" Bob said to the electronic gizmo (unwilling to meet James's eye).

"Who needs an alarm around here with you guys rustling around all night?" Porter complained, loud enough to be heard from the private side of the bathroom door.

"And getting up to *pee* in the middle of the night!" the thirty-one-year-old added.

"I don't have any memory of anyone getting up to pee," Bob said mildly, as every smile line on his face fused into a grin.

"Boy, conversation sure has gone downhill since the girls left," James, the politically correct mailman, chided.

"Muffins up," Sergeant James announced, again.

Sonneborn rose from his chair and moved toward the kitchen (not that the muffin was his).

"Alarm clocks are tricky," Bob said, almost innocently.

James Huntington spun around and eyed him suspiciously.

"How many times did you get up last night?" he challenged.

"About as many times as you hit your snooze button and went back to sleep!" Aaron chided. "Why not just get up on the third ring instead of going back to sleep and going through apnea? Boy, talk about weird breathing."

James looked levelly at his young antagonist but without antagonism. His is a face that moves easily between seriousness and mirth. Suddenly he laughed—a two-part laugh: first part expelled air, then after the diaphragm catches, an infectious cackle.

"Well, nobody could hear me breathing over the snoring," he argued. "Somebody down here was really sawing logs. It sounded like a chain saw convention."

He didn't exactly finger me directly, but the next words out of his mouth were directed at me. "You going to sea watch?"

"Don't think so. Not until it clears a bit."

It was the answer everyone wanted to hear.

If nobody went out, then nobody had to feel bad about staying in.

Nobody who has reached a point in his life when he enjoys his middle-aged comforts wants to be accused of being a "cake eater."

Like Bob said, the barometer was rising. An hour, maybe

two, the rain might be light enough to make birding possible (if not necessarily enjoyable) and a sweep of the boneyards profitable.

Everyone was thinking the same thing. Southwest winds last night. Maybe . . . Maybe . . . Maybe the bird of the trip was out there. Waiting. Going nowhere until the rain died.

Getting late in the migration period for sure, but prime time for buntings. Little or rustic bunting. Maybe the gray bunting everyone's been expecting for years. Maybe.

With rain beating on the windows, everyone settled into a leisurely morning. Lathering bagels with artery-clogging measures of butter (except Dr. Sonneborn). Reading, studying field guides, discussing weighty matters such as alder and willow flycatcher distribution while the morning's third pot of coffee gurgled to fruition.

Everyone was awake now. Everyone engaged in the time-killing things people do while waiting to do what they want to do but are prevented by circumstances from doing it.

Except for rain gear hanging from every available hook and the early hour (and the absence of beer bottles and empty pizza boxes), it looked about like any gathering of male friends.

We could have been sitting in a motel room in South Bend, Indiana, killing time until the 1:00 kickoff of the Notre Dame Irish versus Who Cares game and it would have been the same. We could have been chilling in a waterfront rental in Manteo, North Carolina, waiting for our boat captain to call and give the word that our tuna charter was on, or counting down the minutes until our scheduled tee time at Pebble Beach.

United by shared interest, bonded by friendship, unaffected by the habit-inhibiting influence of women.

It is, in twenty-first-century America, not particularly PC to discuss differences related to gender, even to acknowledge that such differences exist.

Tough.

I'm sure that women, in their own sexually unfettered gatherings, must at times wonder what it is that "the guys" do, or think, or say when removed from their civilizing influence. They may assume, somewhat naturally and perhaps uneasily, that conversation inclines toward them, that female aspects and foibles are coarsely exploited for male merriment.

I can't speak to other gatherings, but here, on Gambell, locker room humor was conspicuously absent, the names of spouses rarely mentioned. It wasn't that the subject of women was taboo. It was just that it didn't much come up.

I don't know whether indifference is better than exploitation, but there you have it.

Another thing that women in general, and wives in particular, might find unnerving was the relative neatness of the place, the order that established itself without anyone giving orders.

Clothes were hung on hooks, not lofted over chairs. Snacks were centralized in one location. Dishes were not lying about (not even stacked, unwashed, in the sink!), and when enough sand or candy wrappers or lens-cleaning tissue accumulated on the floor, someone (and not always the same person) would reach for a broom and a dustpan and just do what was necessary to make the place tidy.

Not painfully tidy. Practically tidy.

And while the language was occasionally colorful . . .

"I think the rain's letting up. Think I'll go over to the Near

Bone Yard to take a quick look; see what the wind's blown in."

"Uh, excuse me, comrade, but there is no 'I' in 'we.' "

"Oh, yeah, well, is there an 'I' in 'Fuck you'?"

"No. But there is in '*Kiss my ass*'!"

. . . the artful use of expletives was done more for expressive poignancy and general merriment than to compensate for linguistic shortcomings.

Maybe it was the absence of alcohol. Maybe it was the concupiscent-leaching effects of maturity. But if I had to guess, I'd say it had more to do with avocational focus. The kind that allows grown men to vault decades and engage the world, once again, with the enthusiasm of the little boys that women throughout the ages have tried and failed to suppress.

A focus that makes a wayward bunting as important and desirable as a 1958 Mickey Mantle baseball card, an Austin-Healey 3000, two tickets to the Super Bowl, and a "marlin on the line!"

It's a hunter-gatherer thing. And frankly, ladies, it is out of your control.

But feel free to discuss it.

"Barometer's still climbing," Bob announced.

Maybe, every mind mused. The bird of the trip. Just a boneyard sweep away.

It's a Bird, Bird, Bird, Bird World

So just what is it about "listing" that would prompt a bunch of otherwise well-adjusted adults to spend their lives chasing birds around a continent when there are perfectly fine birds to find, and enjoy, right at home?

It's a subject I've thought about a lot, and not because I am a particularly avid bird lister/chaser. I'm not. But the passion that birders bring to bear in the name of seeing the next new species is not just remarkable, it is enviable.

And exciting, and challenging, and bonding, and spontaneous and affirming and . . .

Look at birding as a treasure hunt. One great big, lifelong search for nature's most beautiful and inspiring creations.

In a sense it's like collecting shells on the beach. They are feasts for the eyes. Tokens of fortune and achievement. Things to hold and savor (even, in the case of birds, only in your mind).

Except unlike shells, birds have free will. They can hide. They can fly. So birding is not just collecting. It is challenging. A sport! Find the bird and pin a name to it, you win! Bird throws a move on you and you get an unidentifiable view or it skips town before you arrive, bird wins. You lose.

But animation is a two-edged sword, and sometimes it cuts your way. If birds move, they can turn up anywhere, anytime. Every day a birder wakes, he wakes to possibility. Every ring of the cell phone, every text message or visit to a birding listserve might be the clarion call that cuts through daily routine and sends him off on a merry chase.

Imagine a life in which you never know where your head might fall that night. It could be a motel in some corner of the continent you have never been. New sights, new experiences, new friends.

It could be one of a dozen high-scoring vagrant traps that you know and love (and instead of microwave lasagna at home tonight, you'll be eating a platter of beef enchiladas in McAllen, Texas, or chowing down on a pizza steak hoagie at the C-View Inn in Cape May, New Jersey).

With James, or Paul, or Sandy, or Mac, or any one of a number of friends who share your passion (and were also able to adjust their schedules and catch a flight out). Every hot new bird is the catalyst for an impromptu gathering of the clan.

And, yes, listing at this level is not a poor man's game. But James Huntington is one of North America's top players, and while I don't know how much mail carriers make, I'm willing to bet it's not six figures. North America's top lister, Macklin Smith, is a professor of English, and the late Andy Banker, James's mentor, was a retired high school debate coach.

There is also nothing to say that a lister must have a continental scope in order to play and win. Most listers draw their geographic cinches fiscally tight, focusing on state lists, or county lists, or maybe playing within the temporal boundaries of a year list. How many birds can you see in one year, in whatever arena you define? At the end of the year, count up your winnings, erase the slate, start the game anew.

Can you image a life in which you get a clean slate every year? Can you imagine drinking from a cup that will never run dry because every season, every favorable wind replenishes the cup anew? Can you image keeping a treasure chest that gets richer every year, whose wealth will never tarnish, and whose contemplation unlocks a lifetime of encounters and achievement?

Oh, they are very alluring, chasing and listing. Push all our motivational buttons. Bring out the little kid in all of us.

It begs the question why Linda and I are not ourselves avid listers.

The answer is twofold. First, I like birding, but I hate bookkeeping. Second, I simply cannot stand it when I chase a bird and dip (birder talk for "miss the bird").

It's less nerve-racking being on Gambell. Here, all you have to do is wait for new birds to come to you. And for the weather to clear.

The Last Sweep

Blue sky was beginning to appear in gaps between the clouds. There was a peregrine soaring to the north, and the local ravens were tossing black admonishments its way.

We were scattered across the ridge east of town. No order, no discipline. Just a troop of men working their way across the rock- and cross-strewn hillside, hoping the next step would be the one to flush some aspired-to Asian waif. The rocks just came with the terrain. They were natural. The crosses marked the graves of the Yupik ancestors, who were, likewise, part of the terrain and just as natural.

Elsewhere across North America, people were busily going about the matters that engage lives. Here in Gambell, on this blustery day in mid-September, it was no different. A postman, a surgeon, a tour company operator, a writer, and their friends were on the hunt for a flock comprising a fox sparrow, a junco, two Savannah sparrows, and a white-crowned and a golden-crowned sparrow, for reasons that would be hard to explain.

Unless you subscribe to the notion that fun is its own reward. Unless you have discovered that the value of any prize is only as great as the value we ascribe to it.

This was our last full day on the island. Weather permitting, tomorrow's plane would fly us back to the mainland and lives deferred.

I was, on this particular sweep, higher up on the ridge than my companions, and from this vantage they looked very small, like children playing some daring game of capture the flag. Bob, despite his game leg, was also well up on the hill, nearest to me. Dave Sonneborn was about halfway up. The rest of our group was spread out below.

Suddenly everyone picked up the pace. Not running exactly, but not strolling either. If they lowered themselves from boulders instead of jumping, it could have been attributed to wisdom. If they seemed to be favoring one leg over the other when vaulting streams, it wasn't because one knee was bad, it was because the other was better.

Looking ahead, I could see Paul Lehman down near the Far Bone Yard, speaking into the radio, and several more figures pointing and moving up the hill.

Bob, knowing I didn't have a radio, turned my way, cupped his hands around his mouth, and shouted. "Willow warbler."

I waved. Gave Bob a thumbs-up.

Good bird. Really good. Only the third North American record. The reason I knew was that I was present for the second North American record. Saw it two weeks earlier along with the members of the first WBA group (including Linda) but before most of the present company had arrived.

So I didn't scramble to join them. Call it complacency, call it smugness. I prefer to think it was the wisdom of age. There were a lot of slippery rocks and a lot of vengeful gravity between me and the bottom of the hill. Willow warbler is a pretty drab-looking bird, after all, and like I said, I'd seen one before.

So instead of rushing, I stayed high to enjoy the show. Watched how the wave of breathless men merged with those already assembled near the boneyard. Noted how they moved up the hill, then fanned out for a sweep that was interrupted by a shout that brought all at a run.

It could have been the distance, it could have been my aging eyes, but from where I stood, as the press men got closer to their quarry, all signs of the older men I'd spent the week with disappeared. What was left was a host of eager boys racing to be first and desperate not to be late.

None of them was. Everyone claimed the flag. Willow warbler was a life bird for most (including Dave Sonneborn, number 401 for Alaska).

It's a funny thing about games and hobbies. When we're young, they figure so prominently in our lives. Collecting baseball cards, finding birds' nests, playing soccer, going horseback riding or hunting or fishing. Then, for years going on decades, these fascinations get tabled. They make way for education, courtship, and careers; kids, mortgages, and college tuition.

Then one day, after the kids are gone, after the career ladder has been climbed, we wake up and discover we're unfettered again. The games come out, drawn from wherever it is people store the things they love during the busy years. Games to engage us. Games to unite us.

Games that give us a reason to get up in the morning and allow us to greet pillows in the evening with a smile. Games so engaging they can even drive people, literally, to the ends of the earth. No, I'm not the world's biggest lister. But I certainly get the allure, and sometimes, in the right place and the right company, the allure even gets me.

We were halfway through lunch and the embellished recountings of each individual's brave scamper across treacherous terrain when the radio crackled and the voice of Paul Lehman announced, "There is a common rosefinch in the Far Bone Yard."

Common rosefinch! I missed that bird by minutes on Attu, back in 1990. Linda got it; I dipped. She's had that bird on me ever since.

Not that I'm competitive. And a while back, I noted that one of the wonderful things about listing is the enduring luster of your compounded wealth, how the treasured birds you gather will never tarnish in the coffers of your mind. This is true. But what I didn't tell you, and what is equally true, is that it is the treasure still lying on the beach, the birds you haven't seen, that always shines brighter.

If you happen to be birding Gambell and find half a petrified peanut butter sandwich up on a hillside dotted with crosses, it's mine. Look in the direction of "Magic Rock." I think that's where it landed.

If you're a North American birder and haven't got an x next to common rosefinch there's no need to explain.

CHAPTER 7

Moon Month of Amiraijaut (September–October),
"Velvet Peels from Caribou Antlers"

Hunting with Heimo

Coleen River, Arctic National Wildlife Refuge, Alaska

"We'll be sitting over there," Heimo announced, indicating the whereabouts of "over there" with a wave of his ungloved hand. It was cold. Temperature in the single digits. Yet the trapper's words were unclouded; heard but not seen. The parched Arctic air had taken his breath away.

"All right," I acknowledged.

"There's a lake just beyond those trees. Game trails on both sides. I'll come back and see how you're doing after we get settled."

"That's fine," I agreed, noting anxiousness in Heimo's voice.

Seeing, beneath age-lushened eyebrows, the look of worry in his eyes.

I knew he was blaming himself for not finding caribou, and I didn't need to underscore this with the truth that was known to all of us. This was the last day of our six-day hunt. Weather permitting, Bob and I would be flying out tomorrow with or without a cooler packed with caribou.

We'd been hunting both sides of the Coleen for five days now. Five days in one of the most unpeopled parts of Alaska (not to mention the southeastern corner of the Arctic National Wildlife Refuge).

We hadn't seen a caribou. Only cut a single track. Heimo had warned us, when we were planning our hunt, that there were no guarantees. Some years the animals of the Porcupine caribou herd wintered near his cabin, sometimes in neighboring Canada. "You know more people have starved to death waiting for caribou than any other animal," the fifty-three-year-old trapper cautioned.

We did know, or at least accepted the uncertainty. That's why it's called "hunting" and not "killing animals."

Heimo's concern was misplaced for another reason, too. We were friends and guests, not clients. Any personal obligation Heimo felt was unwarranted. But it's funny how hunters, even hunters as experienced as Heimo, find it hard to surrender to the cold, hard reality that effort and ability are sometimes trumped by luck. Unless you don't believe in luck and affirm, instead, the leveraging force of fate. Either way, luck or fate, it's still every hunter's privilege and obligation to go out and meet it. Just as we were doing now.

"I'm going to head out past the place I was sitting the other day," I told him. "Saw a stand of spruce I liked. It will let me glass more ground. You'll know it when you see it."

"Okay," Heimo said, turning, walking in a northeasterly direction. Leaving hip-boot tracks so obvious they could probably be seen from space.

I'd already witnessed Heimo's uncanny ability to detect and decode animal tracks not merely in snow but beneath it. Watched him stop, yesterday, in the middle of a game trail and follow, with his fingers, the buried tracks of a pine marten, showing us where the small weasel had crossed the trail and exited up a bank.

Clearly, *The Final Frontiersman,* as his biography recognizes him, would have no trouble following my trail in the three inches of new snow that had ended just before dawn.

A beautiful snow. A hunter's snow.

"See you later," I said to Bob, whose camouflage hunting jacket had lost much of its off-the-rack newness. "I'll be waiting for your shot."

"Be waiting for yours," he said, smiling, turning, shifting the vintage .30-06 military rifle onto his shoulder. Months earlier, when Bob had decided after sixty-two years and no small amount of soul-searching to go hunting for the first time, he'd taken the rifle to a gunsmith to have it fitted with a rifle scope only to have his request refused.

The rifle, he was told, was a collector's item. Tapping it for scope mounts would destroy its value. If he was willing to trade the gun, he could have his pick of just about any modern hunting rifle in the man's shop.

Bob refused. The gun had been a gift from his late father, a career military officer. Bob wanted to hunt with his father's gun or not at all. That was that and there he was. Walking quickly to catch Heimo. The world's newest caribou hunter armed with an open-sight rifle. It wouldn't have raised the eyebrows of Native peoples, who have, for decades, been using military rifles to good effect, but many sportsmen might have scoffed.

Without basis.

Bob had taken the rifle out on a range a number of times before our trip. Figured he was fine with it to about two hundred yards. Which is, depending again on whether you believe in luck or fate, good news or bad news for caribou. Bad news if caribou believe in luck and a poor shot means you live. Good news if caribou subscribe to the notion of fate, and all any animal can aspire to at the natural end of its life is a quick death.

Me? I have at times subscribed to both schools—i.e., that the universe operates under a rigid system of clockwork predictability and the notion that the universe is a vessel of infinity, random possibility—and I'm not certain, given a universe of infinite possibility, that luck and fate cannot exist side by side (as illogical as that might sound).

I waited several minutes to mark where my companions entered the woods. Picked out a distinctive cluster of trees to the left, making a mental note to direct no shot to the right.

Then, unslinging my customized .280 Remington, I started off in the opposite direction. Heading for the predetermined stand of trees and whatever luck (or fate) would meet me there.

What I very much hoped for was a caribou on the ground. My first. Like Bob, I've never hunted this celebrated Arctic deer. Also like Bob, I came to hunting only after a great deal of deliberation.

WHERE DESTINY MEETS THE HORIZON

It took less time to reach the place than anticipated. Half an hour, with stopping and glassing, but a straight walk would have brought me there in half the time. It was about mid-morning now, by the lie of the sun, which was, on this date—the first of October—and at this latitude, less than 23 degrees above the horizon. The north was losing sunlight at the rate of eight minutes a day now. This, and our desire for good shooting light while we walked in, explains our late start.

The spot I'd selected faced west and offered good visibility north and south. Only east, toward the river and Heimo's cabin, was my view limited by trees. This, and the absence of any caribou sign in that direction, made east the direction I would monitor least.

Winds were light, steady out of the north. Animals coming from that direction or from the west wouldn't scent me. Tucked against the silhouette-absorbing backdrop of spruce, I was pretty nearly invisible.

It was a good spot, conditions favorable. No predator could have asked for better.

The land in front of me was mostly open, tundra dotted with stunted spruce, ground-hugging blueberry and tussock. Four days earlier, when I'd first hunted here, it had been an autumn landscape, rich in reds going to brown. Now, after two snowfalls, it was a canvas primed for winter's full brush. The four inches already on the ground constituted the under-coating. The first snow to fall, it would also be the last snow to melt in the spring. Given the freezing temperatures, what was here was here to stay.

Beyond my stand, about eight hundred yards off, was a protruding finger of forest and beyond it, two, maybe three miles, a rising plain of open, rolling tundra pocked by boulders and trees.

I glassed the near ground, then the far. Searching for the pale forms of grazing animals or dark lines of parallel tracks that mean caribou on the move, finding neither.

Part of me was glad. If I'd spotted caribou out past the trees, I'd have gone for them. But three miles is a long way to portage a couple of hundred pounds of meat (even when the weight is distributed among three). Besides, I much prefer hunting over a strategic crossing point to "still hunting," as walking up on game is unaccountably called.

The only thing my glassing disclosed was a single raven, heading south, and several northern hawk owls that were, as I was about to do, sitting in strategic locations, hunting. Two distant, one close. We'd run into a number of these medium-size, long-tailed northern owls already. Yellow-cheeked vole numbers seemed at their peak. Evidently a goodly number of hawk owls had chosen to take advantage of this bounty and winter in what is, even for these northern owls, the limit of their range.

Choosing a level spot just in front of the largest spruce, leaning my rifle against one of the smaller trees, I shook the snow from the branches and, using my frame pack, scraped the snow down to bare tundra. Snapping off spruce branches, building a mat to keep my seat at least dry, if not warm, I propped the pack up against the tree for a backrest, reached for my rifle, and settled in.

Checking first to make sure everything I might need was in reach: water bottle, binoculars, snacks, laser range finder. Checking next to be certain that the piece of tape I'd put over the muzzle of the rifle was still in place, and that the barrel hadn't become fouled by snow. Checking then to be sure that the rifle scope was also clear, and finally, working the bolt, making doubly sure that I'd remembered to chamber a shell after leaving Bob and Heimo.

Clack. The sound of machined metal on metal was painfully loud in the near silence of the near-winter Arctic. The lubricant-softened glide of the bolt being drawn sounded more akin to a whisper. The slender brass cylinder that winked in the morning sunlight said, Yes, everything is now ready. Two more rounds, snug in the magazine, gave added assurance.

With good luck (or auspicious fate), they would remain there, unused. If my luck was bad, it could go either way.

Clack-clack. I closed the action. Thumbed the safety back, *on.* Laid the rifle across my lap. Just two tasks left. Then I'd be ready.

PICTOGRAPH

The sun was only slightly moved, still short of its midday arch and span. It was a beautiful day, despite the cold. Gray, maybe snowing over the Brooks to the north, but sunny with an ice-crystal-muted blue sky here in the valley.

It looked like more snow tonight. That was a concern. Three inches more and Kirk, our bush pilot, wouldn't be able to land. We'd be stuck until enough snow fell to accommodate skis, and that might take days, even weeks.

Raising my binoculars, mapping a careful search, I struggled to make a mental imprint of the terrain in my mind.

Shadows and trees, rocks and blowdowns. A weathered branch that looked like antlers there. A bush that resembled a shadow-colored animal bedded in the snow over there.

This was my search image. As any predator entering a new area might, I was gaining familiarity with my territory. Any change was something I hoped would draw my eye.

Reasonably confident that no obvious shot was being missed, I exchanged the binoculars for the range finder and, looking out, seeing a spruce that seemed about the right distance, I centered it in the viewfinder, pressed the button, and read the number on the screen.

Two hundred and forty yards. Almost perfect. My rifle was sighted in for 230. At this point, the impact of the bullet would be right where the cross hairs in my scope fell. At this distance, the 150-grain Nosler bullet would be traveling at a zippy twenty-six hundred feet per second and packing a knockdown punch of almost twenty-four hundred foot-pounds of energy. That's plenty for caribou.

When a bullet strikes mass, whether it's a block of gelatin in a ballistics lab or an animal's boiler room, it flattens or mushrooms. Without this engineered deformation, the sliver of metal that is a bullet might pass right through the animal (taking much of the bullet's energy with it), causing damage but not necessarily lethal injury or quick death. When the bullet is expanded, its force is more broadly distributed and absorbed by the body. Quick death from shock, caused by a well-placed bullet, is the objective and hoped-for result.

Why tell you this? First, to make you aware that I am fully aware of the consequences of my action when I train my sights on an animal and direct a bullet that will end its life.

Second, and closely related to this, to impress upon you how seriously I, and all serious hunters, accept the responsibility of that action.

Because the rifle in my hand, which I spend hours on the range practicing with, is capable of killing animals larger than caribou at distances greater than 230 yards. I am not.

When I am shooting from a sitting position, without a rest, I have determined that 230 yards is the limit of my confidence and my skill. The spruce tree, in front of me, was my preset marker. Any caribou I might shoot would have to be closer than the spruce. Or I would have to find a support (a stable limb, my cushioning pack) to steady my aim. Or stalk the animal until I was close enough for confidence.

Or more likely, based upon past experience, I would simply hold my shot and let the animal walk away. I've calculated that even with shots that offer a comfortable degree of confidence, I take one in three.

Why that one? I don't know. It remains a mystery.

So maybe, now, you can better appreciate the final step in my preparation. A ritual I have performed every time I've hunted large game since . . . well, I don't know when. But for a long time.

Reaching for a spruce branch, stripping it of needles, I traced the crude outline of a caribou in the snow. A bull, double-shoveled with sweeping antlers. Too small in the chest, maybe, but, like I said, I'm new to hunting caribou and, to date, have drawn only five—one for each of the preceding days.

I'm better at drawing deer.

Still holding the stick, I touched the pictograph with the

tip, planting it at a point below and behind the shoulder; the place where an animal's life is housed. Then, focusing my mind, I promised to myself, and to the animal, that I would do everything right.

That I would wait until the range was good, and the path of the bullet clear.

That I would not rush the shot.

That I would wait for the calming assurance, the knowing that precedes shots that are true, before putting into motion things that cannot be called back and whose impact will alter the universe, moving life from one side to the other.

I don't know whether other hunters have similar rituals, but I am sure that the thoughts of good hunters are similarly resolved. I'd just completed my mental checklist when my meditation was shattered by what is, in the minds of things that hunt and are hunted, the most riveting sound in the universe.

The sound of a branch parting beneath the weight of an approaching animal.

SNAP

I have never died, not, at least, in the memory of this lifetime, but my belief is that death will result in a broadening of awareness, that my senses and being will expand to engage a universal totality into which the I that was me will dissolve into a seamless, sensory All.

The snap of a branch is the very antithesis of this. It is riveting. In a synaptic flash, it heightens and concentrates every sense you have on a single point. It cancels out the rest of the universe. It brings your being to bear.

Snap. For millions of years, whether you fall into the ranks of hunter or the ranks of hunted, it has meant life and death.

We, as humans, have been and biologically still are both. Several generations of natural estrangement have not been enough to deactivate several million years of evolutionary hot wiring.

My first instinct, as a creature who has been hunted, was to swivel. Perceive the threat. React.

My discipline, as a hunter, was to freeze, reach out with my senses, gain more information, so that, when I did react, it would be with intelligence and directed action.

The sound was behind me and to the right. The direction from which I'd come.

It was loud enough to be heard through the snow. So a large branch, a large animal. There was one likely possibility. A hypothesis to be tested.

I turned my head, slowly, keeping my thumb on the safety of the rifle but leaving it on, seeing Heimo walking my way, following my tracks, his hip-boot-clad legs closing the distance in long strides.

"Anything?" he asked, dropping to his knees, moving his eyes over the horizon. If he noted the drawing in the snow, he didn't mention it (and I doubt he didn't notice).

"Hunting hawk owls," I said, nodding in the direction of the closest keyed-up bird.

Heimo nodded. "We had one over near the lake, too," he said. "Any sign of caribou?"

"No," I said. "Not yet," I added.

Heimo nodded again, his eyes still sifting the near landscape then the hills beyond. A predator's eyes. Set forward, in the front of the face, the way the eyes of predators are. The eyes of animals that are hunted are set on either side of the face, to facilitate detection all around.

"Kirk said that there're twenty thousand animals just be-yond those hills," Heimo reported. "B-between ten and twenty-five miles away."

The woodsman has a slight stutter that becomes evident when he is keyed up. I guessed that the absence of caribou was still weighing on him. And the proximity of caribou, while encouraging, wasn't particularly helpful. Our bush pi-lot had both a vantage and a mobility we lacked. Unless the herd decided to move and move our way, fifteen miles was as good as fifteen hundred.

There wasn't enough snow on the ground to take a snow machine over. Our effort, two days earlier, to go upriver in a motorized canoe had almost ended in disaster when we grounded and took water less than half a mile from Heimo's cabin.

Cold water. The lakes had already frozen over—during our stay. The river was freezing. Dumping a canoe in water like that is nothing to be cavalier about.

"Beautiful day," I said. "Can't think of a better place to watch the sun go around. If no caribou wanders over, well, then I won't make him famous by putting him in a book. His loss."

Heimo looked quizzically at me, not sure whether I was se-rious or not. Animals, to Heimo and all people who hunt to live, are food. There is no distinction. Over dinner, over one of several delicious ways I was served moose, Heimo's wife, Edna, confided that whenever she and Heimo go to a new area—by plane or canoe—the very first question she applies to her surroundings is "What do I see here that is food, and how do I get it?"

Some might consider this a very limited way of looking at the world, and from their own limited perspective they might even call it "primitive." Actually, it is a very real and bonding way, linking people directly to the world around them. Those who think otherwise have the latitude not to be practical, to nurture bonds with living things that are more emotional than physical and spiritual.

I'm not saying this is bad. I am saying it is not natural.

The moose we were eating was killed by Heimo before Bob and I arrived. Quartered with a belt knife, packed out on foot, the animal was hanging from a cross pole in front of the Korths' fourteen-by-fourteen cabin, halfway to the stove-heated wall tent Bob and I were occupying and right next to the cluster of snares and leg-hold traps that Heimo and Edna would soon be setting. The hanging moose was as confidence-building and critical to their survival as the multiple stacks of firewood laid down nearby.

The fruits of hunting are a major part of their diet. Trapping is their economic mainstay. Whereas animal fur was, once, as fundamental to human survival in cold climates as meat, now it mostly serves the vanity of men and women in fur-fashionable places like Greece, Israel, and Russia, and Alaskan tourists who consider wolf skins on the walls of their dens fitting rustic touches.

Is trapping cruel? Maybe. Cruelty is a human standard. You're human. You decide.

Whether trapping is cruel is not a question any animal has ever asked. Cruelty, like mercy, has no standing or bearing in nature. Killed for food, killed to provide warmth, or killed to instill envy, it's all the same to wolves or lynx who, as predators, deal in death every day.

Is trapping justifiable? That is something that depends a great deal upon the justification, doesn't it? To Heimo and

Edna and the three daughters they raised on the banks of the Coleen, the justification is self-evident. To the people who wear fur, you'll have to ask them.

Me? I stopped trapping years ago. Although once I used to set traps for muskrat, fox, and raccoon in the woods and marshes behind my parents' house. Running my traps before school. Skinning and stretching the few animals I caught in the evening. Selling the pelts to a middleman who never gave me more than $1.50 for a large rat or $4.00 for a raccoon.

In good years, when fur prices on the world market are high, Heimo might make twenty-five thousand dollars.

Gross.

Me? I lost money every year. My greatest expense was replacing the traps stolen by neighborhood kids. Still, I trapped because it was an exciting link to the natural world and to America's frontier heritage. I read *Fur-Fish-Game* magazine monthly and dreamed of someday becoming Heimo Korth.

A trapper. Living off the land in the north woods. Independent. Close to nature.

I didn't. I chickened out. It was Heimo Korth, a kid two years younger than I growing up in suburban Appleton, Wisconsin, who was running traps before school and yearning for adventure, who became the Final Frontiersman.

He left Wisconsin in 1975, at the age of twenty, and headed straight to Alaska. Blundered his way into the wilderness. Built a cabin. And when his supplies ran out (like scores of naive and romance-driven kids before him), he engineered a rescue by forming an SOS out of aluminum foil that could be, and luckily was, seen from the air.

Most people would have quit at this point. Maybe Heimo was just stubborn. Maybe terminally naive. Maybe the Fates were out having a beer or decided to just string the crazy white kid along and see how far his luck would carry him. It carried him, ultimately and unaccountably, to the native village of Savoonga, on St. Lawrence Island, where his unbridled eagerness and pluck earned him a place among the 250 Yupik people. For six years, he was tutored by some of the finest hunters evolution has ever honed, hunting polar bears, walrus, seals, bowhead whales, and . . .

He met Edna, a pureblood Yupik, who agreed to accompany Heimo into the bush, to build and live in a cabin on the Coleen River, about 150 miles north of Fort Yukon and in what would later become the Arctic National Wildlife Refuge.

Their residency and subsistence rights grandfathered in, the Korths are the only year-round residents in an area the size of South Carolina. Their nearest neighbor, a seasonal trapper, is fifty miles south. Their umbilical cord to civilization is the gravel airstrip they cleared themselves.

Edna, or miete dahwa, her Native name, brought to the union not only the practical skills of a native Alaskan but the social support all people, maybe especially those independent few who live at the social rim, crave and need. She also gave Heimo three daughters, who were raised in the bush. What goods they purchased and what amenities they had (including school supplies) came from the money generated by trapping.

Two of the girls, Krin and Rhonda are grown now. "Bush kids" living adult lives in Fairbanks.

One, Coleen, went down to play on the banks of her namesake river one day and never returned. Her framed photo is affixed to the wall of the Korths' cabin. And while in recent years Edna and Heimo have taken to living in Fort Yukon during the summer months, they both admit they would have a difficult time leaving, for good, the river and the daughter that became and remain, in their minds, one.

I looked over at Heimo. Taking him in. A suburban kid's dream come true.

Lightly dressed (by my standards). Wearing a stocking wool cap, use-stained barn jacket, and jeans beneath his insulated hip boots. The cap covered a head of dark hair that was thinning quickly. Beneath his coat, poking from his hip, the .44 Magnum that he wears inside the house and out.

Edna's .44 Magnum, actually. Heimo's revolver was in the shop being repaired.

Six feet and solid, he looks a bit like a bushy-eyed, sideburn-sporting Bill Murray. His beard is going gray. His eyes have an intense, puppy-dog eagerness that matches his personality. Whether you've known Heimo for thirty years or thirty seconds, what impresses you most about the man is his pure, unbridled, childlike enthusiasm.

We met in 1990. Bob, Linda, and I were coming off a backpacking trip in the Brooks Range, an adventure recounted in our book *The Feather Quest*. We'd just been dropped off in Fort Yukon by our pilot, Roger, who invited us to crash at his place for the night and radioed ahead for someone to pick us up at the airstrip and drive us to the cabin.

That someone, it turned out, was a big, friendly, eager guy named Heimo, who took one look at our binoculars and blurted, "Are you guys bird watchers?"

Somewhat taken aback by his enthusiasm, and not sure what our answer committed us to, we assured him we were.

"I'm a bird watcher, too!" he said. "Let's go bird watching!"

And we did. Hopped in the back of the pickup. Rode out to the edge of town. Followed Heimo along a dirt track and

watched as the local birding expert pointed out local breed-
ers such as myrtle warbler . . . northern waterthrush . . . slate-
colored junco . . .

The guy was as excited as a little kid showing off his collection of baseball cards and good, too. He wasn't wearing binoculars. And his identifications (if not the dated names) were
spot on.

After eight or ten birds, he paused. Turned somewhat anx-
ious eyes our way and asked: "Am I doing this right?"

We assured him he was.

Now, he was showing me how to hunt caribou.

"I've killed caribou just over there," he said, nodding toward
the western trees.

"You're okay here," he added. I didn't know whether it was
a statement or a question.

"Yeah, fine. Figure I'll spend the day. Wind's good."

"Okay," he said. "I'm going to see how Bob's doing. We'll
probably build a fire later," he confided. "You'll see the smoke."

"I'll look for it. Thanks."

It was actually one of the shortest conversations I'd had
with Heimo, whose mind is as facile as it is inquisitive, as it is
contemplative. In fact, his rapid departure prevented a return
to a conversation we'd had earlier in the week. One I wanted
to explore again with a man whose life is so clearly and naturally wedded to the animals he hunts.

"Have you hunted ducks?" he'd asked the first time we'd
hunted this opening.

"Sure."

"Have you ever wondered why you shoot the bird you do?
How out of an entire flock you pick *that* one."

I never had. And it surprised me that there was a facet

of hunting that I hadn't explored. But the answer seemed straightforward enough.

I started to answer. Opened my mouth to express just-for-mulated causal links relating to proximity, angle, speed, size, color, eye-catching pattern . . . then shut it, realizing, with a start, that while all these things were true, they were also not the reason the muzzle of my gun fell on the bird it did.

Accepting confusion, instead of false certainty, I was brought to conclude, after several days of thought, that I honestly could not say why I choose one bird in a flock over another.

I only know that a choice is made. That it feels certain and natural, not random.

And I am open enough in my thinking to consider a meta-physical possibility when no practical or logical one presents itself. The possibility that there is some bond, or link, or maybe reason that the point of my gun falls upon this bird and not that one or any other.

I just know that in all my years of hunting, and in all my contemplation of hunting, it was a question I'd never asked. The person who posed it to me was the "primitive" person who thinks of animals as food.

HUNTERS

The sun was as high as it was going to get. Its light, falling warm on my face, balanced the cold that was creeping into my boots.

It was also as warm as it was going to get—in the low teens, I guessed. My feet were just going to have to accept that. Cold feet, for as long humans have lived and hunted the northern regions, are the price of admission.

One of the northern hawk owls had worked its way to a tree less than thirty yards away. Sitting at the very top of a spruce, its head moving in swiveling jerks, it looked like an animate Christmas tree ornament, a dark-winged, yellow-eyed angel atop the tree. Studying, intently, the snowy landscape below. Senses alert for motion or sound.

Consummate predators, armed with more pure hunting skill than any human hunter could bring to bear, raptors have always ranked among my favorite birds. We'd been lucky on this trip. Encountered lots. In fact, with so many northern breeding birds already gone, raptors constituted a large, and exciting, percentage of the birds we'd seen.

On our first day, we'd run into a large adult female goshawk. The bird flushed from the ground, landing not far away. When we investigated, we found a dead snowshoe hare, already dressed in its winter white fur, still warm as life. The kill was so recent the bird had yet to feed. We left quickly, sorry to have disturbed the bird but confident it would return.

As much as human hunters, feathered hunters are bonded to their prey.

Heimo's cabin (and his dog, Kenai) was haunted by a particularly territorial boreal owl who made a practice of dive-bombing the 140-pound Akita (who would take undignified shelter in his kennel and bark in protest). The night of our arrival, Bob and I were awakened by the sound of two great horned owls dueting above our tent and the next morning entertained by a Heimo Korth who was near-giddy with excitement.

It marked only the second time in almost thirty years he'd had great horned owls along the Coleen. The Arctic birds, pale unto white, were very obviously a mated pair. Like the hawk owls, they seemed drawn to the bloom of rodents. Maintaining here, at the very limit of the species's range, what must have been a huge territory, the owls had likely shifted their base of operations in accordance with the availability of prey. Heimo and Edna did much the same, rotating among three different cabins to give the populations of fur bearers they trapped two seasons to recover.

On succeeding days, while hunting, we saw late-migrating rough-legged hawk, golden eagle, northern harrier, as well as great gray owl.

Eight raptors (not counting northern shrike and common raven, honorary raptors) out of a total of twenty-four bird species seen. Come winter, the ratio between predatory birds and birds that are prey would be similarly tight, with six wintering raptor species and a maximum of sixteen non.

When it comes to pushing life right to the sustainable edge, you can count on predators to be half a feather's breadth behind their prey. Sometimes the evolutionary refinements that give hunters their edge even allow them to push life's boundary past its natural limits.

When I led my first bird tour to Antarctica and was, as people tend to be, overwhelmed by the vast array of living things, I realized that all the creatures that had managed to gain a toehold on this most inhospitable of continents were predators.

Not most. All.

There are no seed- or fruit- or even insect-eating creatures in a land devoid of seeds, fruit, and insects. The sole source of food is the sea, and from this resource footing, it gave those creatures evolutionarily refined to utilize it the latitude to colonize the land.

The resource is meat. The colonization, by penguins, skuas, terns, gulls, and assorted nesting seabirds, extends, in some cases, one hundred or more miles inland.

Because I was taught to believe that plants and primary consumers form the base of life's pyramid and are therefore life's all-important foundation, the realization that predators are the colonizing shock troops of life came as a pyramid-tipping surprise.

In retrospect, I don't know why I was surprised. After all, it was the hunters and trappers who pushed first into the American West. Farmers, whose lives are wedded to plants, came later.

A sound, or movement, in a snow-shrouded cluster of blueberries near my feet drew my eye. A yellow-cheeked vole, its namesake cheeks showing, bolted from cover, ran two feet, and disappeared, once more, into the snow.

The owl, looking the other way, saw nothing—or, more correctly, was distracted by other possibility. As I watched, it dropped from its perch, silent as a suspended breath, and fell talons first into the snow.

It lifted off. Talons empty. Took another perch.

Several minutes later the owl stooped again. Once again, finding nothing in its talons more gratifying than snow.

Probably a young bird, I surmised. Hunting for the first time in snow. There were plenty of voles around. Plenty of owls, too. Not a coincidence. The dynamic linking predator and prey makes them partners. What moves one moves the other.

Both partners lead; both partners follow. The universe calls the tune. Life and death join hands, and the circle goes round and round.

It doesn't get more natural than this. Or more real.

The owl flew closer now, taking a perch less than fifty feet away. Seeing me. Dismissing me. Prompting me, maybe, to take sides, even though, as a bystander, I had no standing.

"Hark! the herald angels sing," I sang to the vole, who I figured must still be in the vicinity. "Dark angel," I added. "I'd keep my head down if I were you."

The owl, hearing my voice, turned yellow eyes my way.

The vole? Couldn't say. But two minutes later, the owl flew off, the vole had not emerged, and what might have happened became what didn't happen, which is, after all, not the exception in hunting but the norm. "More people have starved to death waiting for caribou than any other animal," I heard Heimo say, once again, in my mind.

But I wasn't going to starve. Not today, anyway. Edna was working up a batch of chili for tonight. Moose chili. The thought of it made my stomach purr in anticipation, and the granola bars sitting in my pack were reduced to a poor substitute. In one week's time, moose had vaulted to the very top of my epicurean ladder, eclipsing venison, which has, for many years, held first place in my esteem.

Better than barbecued beef. Better than turkey with all the trimmings. Better than lamb or pork or fish; or horse or dog or guinea pig or monkey or murre or long-tailed duck or any other protein centerpiece that human societies wrap meals around.

Oh, yes. And absolutely better than tofu.

So I hunt in order to eat? No. That's as wrong as saying I hunt in order to kill.

Linda and I eat deer because, like the bloom of voles that

had drawn the volume of hawk owls, they are abundant enough in twenty-first-century New Jersey to be depended upon (providing you have the time to dedicate and the skill to hunt them successfully). They are more economical, pound for pound, than even feedlot-raised beef.

It costs me $28 for a New Jersey resident firearm hunting license, which entitles me to two deer. Even if I take two one-and-a-half-year-old white-tailed bucks, weighing, dressed, approximately 110 pounds, and not something in the two-and-a-half-year-old, 145-pound class, I'm still going to trim about 100 to 120 pounds of very usable meat off those animals (50 to 60 pounds each). Even if I choose to have those deer professionally butchered (which, in the name of maintaining the pristine integrity of Linda's kitchen, not to mention matrimonial harmony, I commonly do), the total cost of putting two deer in the freezer comes to $1.58 per pound.

When is the last time you saw ground chuck (much less loins, chops, steaks, ribs, and roasts) for that?

Being environmentalists, we also eat venison because it is more energetically efficient and environmentally friendly than meat (or even produce) in the store.

Very probably you have never stopped to calculate the real, cumulative energetic price tag that stretches back from the grocer's shelf to the item's point of origin. Lamb raised in New Zealand and beef raised in Argentina are shipped here. Asparagus grown in Chile and tangerines grown in Israel are flown here. Add to this the cost of transportation to the slaughterhouse, processing, packing, distribution, and the fuel you, the consumer, expend getting to the store.

The deer I take every year walk up to me. The energetic

cost, per deer, is, on average, four tanks of gas (I hunt some distance from home, and it takes multiple trips to kill two deer), plus the energy and material used by a local butcher, plus the energetic cost of the production and discharge of two twelve-gauge Lightfield two-and-three-quarter-inch slugs.

The energetic production cost of my Remington 11-87, now over twenty years old, has long since been amortized.

As for agriculture, and its energetic and environmental impact . . .

Modern agriculture has accomplished its celebrated productivity at the cost of millions upon millions of acres of what was, once, natural habitat. Habitat that sustained thriving ecosystems supporting a rich and complex mix of plants and animals and who knows how many billions, even trillions of living things.

Some of it was mature hardwood forest that was cut and burned. Some of it was native prairie that was turned and disked. More and more of it is tropical rain forest falling in advance of the plow. All of it was natural. All of it supported a wealth of living things. Almost all that was logged and turned is now gone.

High-intensity, single-crop agriculture strips the land. Changes the soil composition through mechanical manipulation and the addition of growth-boosting chemical fertilizers (most of which enter the water table). Necessitates the multiple and varied applications of insecticidal and fungicidal and herbicidal chemicals (which also enter the water table).

All this requires an enormous cost in fossil fuel consumption. It has resulted, in many places, in the serious depletion of fossil water reserves. It has cost you, the taxpayer, lots and lots of money, because a fair measure of agriculture in the United States is subsidized.

This is not to say that some wildlife—most notably waterfowl and other seed- or grain-eating species, which consume waste grain, and deer and other animals that enjoy cereal grains as much as humans do—has not benefited from agricultural practices. Nevertheless, those cornfields in Nebraska that are a boon to migrating cranes and wintering waterfowl do not, in any compensatory way, come close to supporting the wealth of animals that thrived on the prairies before they were supplanted by agriculture.

I applaud those who embrace a vegetarian lifestyle. Because of its low-impact ambition and, yes, because of its ethical concern for animals. Surprised? You needn't be. Just as politics right and left resemble each other at their opposing extremes, hunters and vegetarians have, at their core, the same motivational regard. Both have modified their lives to embrace other living things. Both care greatly enough about wildlife to defend it. Both share a reverence for life.

But if you are a vegetarian because you think that buying vegetables in your grocery store is making life better for wildlife or minimizing your impact on the earth's environment, sorry. Think again. Unless you are putting up your own organically grown produce, you are a shareholder in the earth's growing environmental debt, and you are helping to pull the habitat out from under wildlife.

Linda and I, by consuming two deer—New Jersey–grown and naturally fed—per year, are much more friendly toward and respectful of the environment than anyone whose life is dependent upon a store-bought subsistence.

But having made my case, and saying nothing that is not true, I have one more thing to add.

Being earth-friendly isn't why I hunt either.

ENDLESS HIGH NOON

At this latitude, in late September, the sun seems to hang in the sky. Not rising, not falling, just tracing a course that hugs the horizon. Noon lingers almost to nightfall.

A raven, flying with slow, measured wingbeats, came up from the south, navigating a course that would carry it over the distant wall of trees. For days now, ravens had been coming to investigate my bright orange cap. This one ignored me, but when it drew abreast, it suddenly turned and started circling. Half a mile away, its call, underscoring its curiosity, reached me as it began its second circle.

Aaaah raah.

It sees something there, I thought; I knew. Hunters, even more than most birders, come to appreciate and heed the actions of wildlife. I've had perched hawks disclose to me the presence of high-circling birds beyond the reach of my unaided eyes. Seeing turned heads, drawing a bead on the corner of sky they studied, then training binoculars there, I've found more than one eagle and peregrine with their assist.

While hunting, I've noticed that the normal conversational vocalizations of small birds increase in substance and volume when large animals (like people, like deer) move through.

So I watched the raven and glassed the woods below it. Finding nothing. Ten minutes later a second raven traced the same course, and this one, too, paused and circled. Again, nothing. But it was a place to remember. A place to keep a watchful eye on.

Not, of course, that ravens prey upon caribou, not healthy, living caribou anyway. Ravens are like humans who do not kill their own meat: carrion eaters.

I watched the raven because ravens are commonly the first to see things in lands where any living, moving thing might mean opportunity for a raven. There was something there. Perhaps a bear sleeping near a kill. Perhaps caribou walking this way, flushing voles as they walked.

The hawk owl, shifting perches now at the rate of a new tree every thirty seconds, was faring no better than I was, and, while I am not defeatist, my mind was beginning to stalk the high probability that the trip would end with no caribou.

It was past midafternoon. The sun was weaker. The wind was still. Only a couple more hours of good shooting light. The shifting sunlight was transforming the landscape. Turning weather-bleached blowdowns into full-racked caribou; transmuting the shadow-colored forms of possible bedded caribou into shadow-cloaked boulders.

Every pass of the glass fell on new possibility. Every possibility, under scrutiny, turned to clay. Boring? Disappointing? No. Simply hunting.

Suddenly, my senses went on full alert. No. Not caribou. Smoke. Coming from the trees where Bob and Heimo had disappeared. In the absence of caribou, a warming fire and friendly conversation aren't bad substitutes. Part of me, mostly my feet, thought it a capital idea.

Still . . . still . . . there was good light, still time. Chances were, in this life, I would never again be treated to this near-perfect landscape, marred only by the absence of caribou.

The vole was suddenly back. Darting from and disappearing back into a Lilliputian blueberry thicket. Squeaking loudly enough to be heard by the owl, who, nearly a hundred yards away, dropped from its perch, leveled out just above the ground, and lofted atop the spruce it had used before.

The vole appeared again . . . scampered right toward me. Followed almost immediately by another. Passing me, the preoccupied *Microtus* darted into the skirt of tree branches within arm's reach. The owl flew in, took a perch on the tallest spire above my head, and, turning his eyes down, studied first the place the voles had disappeared. Then me. Then the snow again.

"Not my type," I said to the bird. "You've got first dibs."

The bird wasn't troubled by my voice or my presence. Wearing camo, being still, I'm habitually investigated by birds and other animals when I hunt. On multiple occasions I've had chickadees land on the barrel of my gun. Several times I've had flying squirrels scramble along the length of my body, and, once, a raccoon whose eyes were level with mine reached with an exploring paw to see what manner of creature shared its tree.

But northern hawk owls are at the extreme end of the scale when it comes to indifference to humans. Some hunters might call them stupid. An animal rights proponent might call them trusting. Me? I think that the animal, which had certainly been aware of me all day, had simply concluded I posed no threat and treated me as it would any other large Arctic creature with whom its life was tangential, not conjoined.

The owl finally flew off, and I was secretly glad. As a colleague, a fellow hunter, I probably should have been rooting for the bird. But I was secretly cheering for the voles, who, like all living things, are entitled to their time on this planet and who, like most wild things, are destined, at some point, to become food for another.

If not today, then tomorrow. Or next week. Or maybe, if they are lucky or it's their fate, sometime in December. But at some point the life path of the vole and the path of another animal would cross and they would become one.

Was there anything that distinguished me from the owl?

Once again, it depends upon perspective and who you ask.

Ask me, I'd say no, except to admit that I am nowhere near the hunter the owl is.

Were the question posed to someone who is opposed to hunting, chances are he would find a good deal of difference, according to the owl the right to hunt because, being an animal and a predator, it must in order to survive but denying me that option because, being human, I am held to a higher ethical standard and because, having nutritional alternatives, I am not forced to kill other living things in order to survive.

I hope I've stated this position correctly. Not being opposed to hunting, I'm not positive that I understand the logic, but being human I think I at least understand the emotive foundation. Fact is, I haven't always been a hunter. For over a decade, I stopped hunting for both practical and philosophical reasons. It was never that I decided hunting is wrong. It just wasn't, for that period, right for me. It was a time in my life when I was too busy to hunt seriously, and hunting is something I take too seriously to do poorly.

I've already addressed the subject of nutrition. Why it makes ethical sense, from an environmental standpoint, to hunt. As for the question of killing animals—the matter of life and death that stands between those who hunt and those who decry it . . .

I guess I should begin by saying how close to the anti-hunting, sometimes called "animal rights" position I am. I think that life is one of the most extraordinary facets in the universe. Anyone who would end a thing's life callously or for amusement is beyond my comprehension.

One time I was interviewed by a Colorado newscaster who did a weekly radio show on the outdoors. He was pleased to learn that I was a hunter, as well as a birder, and in our discussion he mistakenly referred to me as a "sportsman." I corrected him.

"I'm not a sportsman. I'm a hunter."

He was perplexed. The term, in hunting circles, is generally regarded with favor, denoting someone whose approach to hunting is principled and conducted in accordance with governing rules, just as sports are so regulated.

But sports are games. Anything that involves the death of a living thing is not a game, not to me. Of course I hunt legally. But I kill nothing for "sport."

Another time I was invited to write an essay about hunting for *Wildlife Conservation* magazine, the publication of the New York Zoological Society. I don't know what they expected, but what they got was a balanced analysis that came out, in the end, pro-hunting. It was enough to prompt a review by the full staff of editors, whose comments were referred to me.

One of those comments chilled me then. It chills me now. And I think it speaks, if not to the reason many intelligent, sensitive, and well-intentioned people are opposed to hunting, then at least to the gulf of misunderstanding that exists between hunters and non-hunters.

Said this individual, this editor, from her estrangement, "Oh, I get it. It [hunting] is like playing predator."

How, I wondered, could anyone call an interaction that results in the death of a living thing "play"? Hunting is not *"playing"* predator. Hunting is *being* predator. If this is how non-hunters perceive hunting, small wonder the gulf is so wide.

END OF DAYS

The sun was riding the crest of the distant hill now. This day was ending like the five before, without caribou. Still, dawn and dusk are peak activity periods for wildlife. It would be premature to call it quits while there was still good shooting light. Irresponsible, even disrespectful.

The thought of a warm fire was growing in my mind. Anticipation of comparing notes, and the day's experiences with Bob and Heimo, enticing. Knowing that they were probably getting curious about my long absence and that one, or both, might be compelled to leave the fire and check up on me made me feel guilty.

I knew I'd leave soon.

The owl, too, was still hunting, changing perches frequently. Doing what hunters the world over do, but, unlike me, whose hunting is limited by regulations to the hours of daylight, the bird would hunt all night, until it was successful.

Until somewhere on the tundra before me and at some pivotal moment in time, the lives of two living things would become one.

A little earlier I asserted that my desire to hunt has nothing to do with a desire to kill or even to live in an environmentally responsible way. What I didn't do is tell you why I *do* hunt.

First, because, in this day and age, I can. The stage, the natural environment, is supportive; the animals, coparticipants in the drama that is hunting, abundant enough to support the activity.

As a drama goes, there is nothing more engaging or real than that which occurs every moment of every day, on a world stage, between animals that hunt and those that are hunted (and among all the earth's creatures, this excludes precious few). As a conservationist and an environmentalist, I'm an avid supporter of this theater. As a birder, I'm an omniscient viewer, delighting in the natural setting, the skill of the actors, and the drama that unfolds.

But when I am hunting, I excuse myself from the audience. Become an actor in the drama itself. There are many things I do in my life that have meaning or merit. Hunting is the most real thing I do.

But even this does not explain why I hunt, and the answer is I don't know, not completely. I was asked, once, by a friend who was not a hunter, and who was surprised to learn that I was, what I "got" from hunting. And it might be because she framed the question this way that an answer came to me.

"I'll tell you," I said. "But only on the condition that you accept that I believe what I say is true. I'm not asking you to believe it yourself. I'm just asking you to believe that I believe."

She nodded her head yes.

"Communion," I said to uncomprehending eyes.

And I wonder, too, as I have wondered since Heimo raised his question with me, why it is when I align my being along the barrel of a gun that falls so naturally, or maybe supernaturally, upon this animal and not that, whether it is luck, fate, or something else altogether that directs and draws my aim.

I know, and affirm, that the communion between predator and prey does not die with the dying. The question is, does the communion exist before the shot, as I believe Heimo was implying? And if it does, is it really, then, my will that brings about that shot, as I have, perhaps, in arrogance always assumed? Or is it the will of two?

Somewhat stiffly, I levered my fifty-seven-year-old frame to a stand. Collected my things and stowed them in my pack. Took one last look around. Considered ejecting the cartridge from my rifle, but . . .

Bringing the gun to my shoulder, I could still see, clearly, the cross hairs of the sight against the snow and, even, the darkening trees.

Luck favors the prepared.

Fate is fickle, not stupid.

Communion? Takes two. But my responsibility extends only to the governance of one. I left the cartridge where it was.

The owl was still there as I started toward the trees. Still hunting.

CHAPTER 8

Moon Month of Ukiulirut (October–November),
"Winter Starts"

The Polar Bear's Picnic

Churchill, Manitoba

The party was in full swing, fueled by the success of an expedition exceeding anyone's expectations and the understanding that this was our last night together. Five days of in-your-
face, shoot 'em until your memory cards are full encounters
with polar bears had cemented our group with good feeling
and friendship.

When the members of our photography tour had first convened, six days earlier, in the airport hotel in Winnipeg, it had
been all about posturing and pecking order.

Who'd been where. Who'd been published. Who had the

newest pixel-packed DSLR or the biggest and fastest-shoot-
ing lens. Now, it was all about shared experience and exchang-
ing e-mail addresses and assurances that best images would
soon be posted on Web sites for everyone's viewing pleasure.

Without anyone noticing, I excused myself from the party.
Took my plastic wineglass out of the dining car, through the
adjoining sleeping cars, and onto the outside deck of our Tundra Buggy, docked, now, at a right angle to the famed Tundra
Buggy Lodge.

For more than twenty years, visitors from all over the world
have used this ingenious hotel on wheels as their jump-off
point for what must rank as one of the greatest ecotourist adventures on the planet: the latitude to get up close and personal, in safety and comfort, with the largest land carnivore
on the planet. Every year, in late October and early November,
approximately thirteen thousand visitors are shuttled through
Churchill, Manitoba's tourism infrastructure and come, literally, face-to-face with the animal that is the poster child for
one of the planet's last, great unsullied and most threatened
biomes.

That biome is the polar ice sheet. The land that is not. Cir-
cumscribing the entire northern portion of the earth. Crossing
all time zones and embracing Asia, Europe, Greenland, and
North America. Retreating in the northern summer, advancing beneath the dark Arctic winter, by early November, winter's transforming touch reaches 58 degrees, 46 minutes north
latitude, where the shipping port of Churchill and the south-
western shores of Hudson Bay lie. Stranded onshore, waiting
for winter to turn seawater into navigable ice, are scores of polar bears—most of whom have been grounded for months.

The Tundra Buggy Lodge is parked right where the bay

freezes first, and bears gang up waiting for the ice to form. Twenty-five miles (or an hour-and-a-half Tundra Buggy ride) east of Churchill, two hundred yards south of Hudson Bay, and right at the northern edge of the taiga forest, it's an eco-tourist extravaganza to humble all others at the "Polar Bear Capital of the World."

Zipping my North Face jacket to my throat, leaning my elbows on the metal sides of the outside deck, I took a sip of wine (before it froze) and started searching the skies of the moon month of Ukiulirut, in the season Ukiaksaaq.

Ukiaksaaq, encompassing late October and early November, means "autumn" in the language of the Inuit. *Ukiulirut* means, literally, "winter starts." One of the environmental markers signaling the onset of Ukiulirut is the initial formation of sea ice. Ukiaq, or "early winter," is heralded by frozen seas and a resumption of seal hunting by sled dog teams on the ice.

The same ice and seals that the bears were waiting for.

Linda and I wouldn't be here for Ukiaq. Neither would the bears. They would be out on the ice until late Upirngaaq, spring—the season that was waxing into summer when, many pages ago, you opened this book.

Overhead was the constellation Tukturjuit, "caribou," although you may know it better as the Big Dipper. Also visible was Uqsuutaattiaq, the "seal oil lamp" in which westerners, looking at the W-shaped configuration, find the likeness of Cassiopeia, the long-dead Ethiopian queen.

Just visible in the western sky was the bright star Sivulliik, the "first one," part of the three-star constellation that bears the same name. Sivulliik's appearance in September signals the onset of real autumn, and it remains one of the brightest stars in the Arctic night during the winter months.

The legend that goes with the constellation involves an old man who killed his brother-in-law, the murderer's nephew (whom the old man taunts), and a grandmother who comes to the boy's rescue after the boy screws up his nerve and accuses his uncle of the crime. For his boldness, the lad finds the old man chasing him around the igloo with a knife. In the sky, as in the legend, the three stars of Sivulliik are chasing one another.

Westerners know the star as Arcturus, the fourth brightest star in the heavens. Muphrid, like Arcturus, is a star in the constellation known as the Herdsman. And Vega is the fifth brightest star in the heavens and part of the constellation known as the Lyre.

Human cultures project into the night sky what they know on Earth. Herdsmen and stringed instruments are alien to the Native people of the North, but violence and death are not. In fact, much of Inuit cosmogony may seem, by western standards, obsessively dark. Dark or not, it is reflective of a people nurtured by an environment in which death is never far away and mercy means a quick end, not surviving to die another day.

The Inuit legend behind the constellation Nanurjuk underscores this harsh reality. As this story goes, a woman who miscarried fled her husband and found shelter in the company of bears, who treated her kindly and caught seals for her to eat. Growing lonely, the woman asked to visit her family but was told not to mention the fact that she lived with bears or to disclose their location.

The woman made the promise but broke it, and when the adult bear saw the sleds of hunters approaching, the bear showed compassion for her young by biting them to death so that they would not fall under the power of men. Then she raced to the house of the woman and bit her to death (and not from compassion).

The bear tried to escape but was pursued by dogs, who surrounded her in a semicircle. Suddenly the bear and her attackers were lifted into the sky, where they appear today, as the star group known to westerners as the Pleiades in the constellation Taurus. The very brightest star in the cluster, Alcyone, is the bear. The encircling lesser stars, the dogs.

At this latitude, Nanurjuk would not appear in the sky for several hours. It was, nevertheless, a beautiful night at the trailing end of autumn and the onset of the "great darkness." Having oriented myself in time and space, I lifted the glass first to toast the stars, then to my lips. Raised my head, filling my mouth with Chardonnay slush. Lowered the glass and, looking down, found myself face-to-face with the business end of a polar bear whose snout was about two and a half feet from my own. The animal was standing on his hind paws, with his front paws pressed against the sides of the porch. He was looking up at me with polite intensity. Six to seven hundred pounds of bear as close as a front-seat passenger in a midsize sedan, and I hadn't heard a thing.

I wonder how many ringed seals have enjoyed just this image for their last mortal sight, the cerebral part of my brain mused.

How could anything so big move so silently? a deeper, more basic portion of my brain more or less asked. But the formulation of this thought was difficult insofar as it had to work its way past a cold, dark knot of fear that was squeezing the base of my brain.

"Once we board the Tundra Buggy," our tour leader, Rob Day, had chanted the day we arrived in Churchill, "your feet won't touch the ground until we're back in Churchill."

I was somewhat miffed by the restriction at the time. Found myself a good deal more philosophical about it now.

NOSE TO SNOUT

The bear wasn't aggressive. He appeared, in fact, to be benignly curious—an adaptive trait that many predators in places where food is often scarce have in common. Something new or different might be something to exploit, and something to exploit might mean food.

And it wasn't like the bear had never leaned up against a Tundra Buggy before. We, after all, had enjoyed five days of encounters like this one and the bear, a young male, probably three or more seasons' worth.

It was the suddenness, not the intimacy, that was shocking; and the incredible stealth that has made the polar bear one of the most accomplished hunters on the planet. Able to hide in a landscape where there is no place to hide; stalking prey so wary that the mere sight of a human a quarter mile away sends sunning seals squirting into their air holes.

My first instinct . . . well, let's forget my first instinct. My second instinct was to go back to the bar for Linda, so we could share our own private polar bear.

But like I said, we'd already had five successful days of shooting. There wasn't a photographer in the lot who hadn't filled their memory cards five times over (and some had probably maxed out the hard drives on their laptops, too).

So I decided to just keep this bear to myself. Enjoy a little intimacy with the poster child of the North. Linda and I had experienced a great many wonderful things since that first trip out to the edge of the winter ice sheet way back in June—about the time this male bear was coming ashore in Churchill. We were ending our adventure. He was just starting his. And I?

I was just trying to fit all the memories and encounters into some sort of cognitive framework (which is the gift, and curse, of humanity).

"Hi," I said. "I'll bet you're hungry."

At the beginning of summer, all the polar bears of Hudson Bay must come ashore. Being creatures of the ice, specialized to hunt seals, whose lives orbit between the ice above and the rich waters of the continental shelf below, when the ice melts, bears head inland and hole up in dens excavated in permafrost, where they, very literally, put themselves on ice.

In temperatures over fifty degrees Fahrenheit, polar bears overheat. So during the summer months they chill and fast. In other places, like the Chukchi Sea, bears retreat with the ice, remaining out on the permanent icecap all year (females even give birth to their young on the ice).

This young male bear, like the fifty or so bears in the area, was moving headlong into the coming season and habitat it was superbly suited for.

"You snuck up on me from under the bus, didn't you?" I accused.

The bear lifted his longish nose a little higher in my direction but otherwise didn't rise to the challenge. Not that it mattered. Bear had me dead to rights, fair and square. Used the cover of the lodge and my inattentiveness to advantage. Snuck up on me, another hunter. If I'd been on the ground, or if Tundra Buggies were built three feet lower, my spirit would be on the way to Quilak, Inuit Heaven, in time for scrimmage under the northern lights that were just beginning to shimmer.

Lucky for me polar bears aren't high jumpers and the folks who convert old school buses into Tundra Buggies take into account both the reach of bears and the inattentiveness of ecotourists.

It's unlikely the bear had been waiting under the bus—a technique they use to capture seals. Smelling a seal's breathing hole from over a mile away, the bears maneuver into position and wait for the mammal to surface for a quick breath, dispatching it with a smashing blow of the paw or plunging jaws attached to a long, heavily muscled neck.

The long-snoutedness of polar bears is one of the anatomical refinements bequeathed to the animals when polar bears split off from brown bears some 250,000 years ago. Other refinements include size. Adult male polar bears weigh between 880 and 1,500 pounds (about twice the size of a Siberian tiger or your average grizzly bear); females average half the weight of males. Large body mass helps conserve heat in cold environments. Size is also an advantage when securing and leveraging prey.

Ringed seals, weighing about 140 pounds, constitute polar bears' primary prey. But the bears have also been known to kill adult walrus weighing twice as much as an adult bear and even beluga whales. Augmenting the bear's front-end strength and muscular neck are long, sharp canine teeth, sharp-edged "grinding teeth" specialized for a meat diet; short but very sharp claws; and the pads on their oversize feet are shod with small, soft papillae that provide suction-cup traction on ice.

The entire battle chassis is camouflaged in long, translucent fur that can appear white to yellowish. This outer layer of guard hairs covers a dense mat of fur and, beneath that, nearly four inches of blubber for bears in prime condition. So little heat is lost from this multilayered, insulating package that, even on ice, polar bears are difficult to detect with infrared sensors, and the animals quickly overheat, even in subzero temperatures, after running little more than a mile. The average cruising speed of a polar bear on land is between three and four miles per hour. At sea they can make six miles per hour and have been recorded more than 150 miles from ice or land.

If you have wondered why polar bears are classified by experts as marine mammals, this, and their near dependence upon marine prey, is why.

While they are almost wholly carnivorous, it is not, strictly speaking, accurate to call polar bears "meat eaters." The preferred food of polar bears is fat. Adult bears eat little else. Cubs, who need protein for growth, and younger, inexperienced bears, who get muscled off kills by older larger bears, commonly or more commonly dine on seal meat.

Despite their predatory predilections, the faces of polar bears are hardly frightening. In fact, their button black eyes, black noses, and short, cubbed ears make them as winsome as pandas and almost as endearing as harp seal pups (whose snow-white fur is very probably a defensive adaptation against polar bears—seal pups in the bear-free Antarctic are dark).

Admittedly, older males, whose faces are scarred from battles with other males, score low on the oh-so-cute register. But the face of the animal in front of me was winsome enough to draw a petting hand. It looked, in fact, just like the big stuffed polar bear I once saw (and coveted) on the floor of an F.A.O. Schwarz toy store—right down to the price tag stuck in its ear.

A bright white numbered tag, denoting a bear that had been captured, measured, and subjected to assorted indignities by researchers striving to learn more about the health and stability of polar bear populations. What they are learning is that the populations of several bear groups are declining, that their average weight is dropping, and that the survival rate of cubs is plummeting. In sum, the future for polar bears looks bleak.

"I see you've met representatives from my species before," I soothed. The bear drew back (perhaps surprised at my prescience) but continued to look me square in the face.

After a lifetime spent engaging the natural world, I've looked into the eyes of a lot of animals. I don't think I've ever seen eyes so benignly intense. It was hard to believe I was staring into the face of an animal that could dispatch me with the flick of a paw. And if there was more justice in the universe, the creature could probably do so with immunity. Fact is, polar bears don't have a great deal to thank our species for, and what good feelings they might harbor are shrinking fast.

Literally.

WHERE SPECIES COLLIDE

For tens of thousands of years, polar bears pretty much had the Arctic marine environment to themselves. Diverging from brown bears after a period of glacially enforced separation, polar bears took an evolutionary tack that converted them from land-based omnivores into icecap-dwelling carnivores.

This period, characterized by recurring intervals of warming and glaciation, also saw, and perhaps spawned, an evolution within our own hominid ranks. During this period, Neanderthal man evolved from *Homo erectus,* a protohuman whose origin was the temperate equatorial zone. Neanderthals, who ranged from western Asia across Europe to the British Isles, were, like polar bears, structurally modified to withstand cold. Their body and muscle mass were greater than those of our human species. Their brains, too, were on average larger than our own, serving not only to "drive" the flesh-and-bone machines but to aid Neanderthals in what must have been, in their glaciated habitat, nearly a full-time job: hunting for food.

Like polar bears, Neanderthals were meat eaters, and, like polar bears', their favored prey often exceeded Neanderthals in size. Neanderthals' countermeasure was an intellect that facilitated the manipulation of materials into tools that served as artificial claws and fangs and allowed groups of hunters to plan and coordinate attacks.

Despite their convergent traits and competitive behavior, there is no evidence that Neanderthals and polar bears ever met. That encounter was left to our species, Neanderthals' successors, when, approximately eighteen thousand years ago, human hunters, presumed to have originated in Central Asia, emigrated to Siberia. These early aboriginal peoples then migrated east across the Bering land bridge and may have reached Alaska as early as twelve to fourteen thousand years ago.

Very little is known about these Paleo-Eskimo except that they did, in fact, have toolmaking technology and they very certainly met up with polar bears, as did subsequent waves of northern peoples, the Dorset and Inuit. Polar bears infused themselves into the lives and cultures of these people, and it has even been suggested that the Dorset seal-hunting techniques and igloo-building technology derived from the study of their bruin neighbors.

Eskimo peoples, as semimarine predators, competed directly with polar bears for seals. They may or may not have set out in a deliberate or systematic fashion to hunt polar bears, but they most certainly did have the tools and the techniques to confront and kill polar bears at opportunity or need. Hunting Nanook was nothing a true Eskimo hunter would shirk from. In fact, a man raised in a hunting culture who was presented with the challenge of besting the earth's largest carnivore would relish the confrontation.

As mentioned, in Inuit culture, the Pleiades cluster represents a bear brought to bay by a semicircle of dogs. In some parts of the North, the three stars of Orion's Belt are held to represent hunters racing to join the dogs and kill the bear.

Just as is represented in the sky, Eskimo hunters used dogs to distract the bears, who were then killed with arrows or lances. All parts of the animals were used (except the liver, which because of its high vitamin A content, is toxic). Nanook was not only a worthy adversary but an important part of Eskimo culture—considered a creature that was both spiritually powerful and closely related to humans. Other hunting cultures, having noted the anatomical similarities between humans and the skinned carcasses of bears, have drawn similar conclusions.

So great a respect did Eskimo hunters have for Nanook

that they commonly believed the only way a hunter could kill a bear was for the bear to be a willing accomplice. The bear would have to allow itself to be killed, and such an honor was bequeathed only to a hunter who was worthy.

Eskimo hunters' impact upon polar bear populations was negligible. Eskimo hunters were numerically few, their access to the Arctic environment limited, and, while their hunting skills were advanced, their weapons were primitive. It took a whole other culture to tip the balance and put polar bear numbers on a downhill slide. This would be western culture. In the fourteenth century, polar bears began being killed for their fur in Russia. As human populations grew, and firearm technology improved, the body count mounted until, by the beginning of the Victorian period, hundreds of animals per year were being killed in northern Europe alone.

But it was the twentieth century that saw the greatest slaughter. The ballistics breakthroughs that so effectively eliminated millions of humans in two world wars increasingly came to be trained on bears. Enhanced mobility through the use of aircraft, icebreakers, and, later, snow machines gave the easily winded animals no place to run or hide.

Following World War II, increased hunting pressure from now well-armed indigenous peoples, sports hunters, and military personnel living in Cold War–spawned bases on both sides of the Iron Curtain accelerated the slaughter. Churchill was home to one such outpost, a Strategic Air Command bomber base. As one bear biologist expressed it to me, "Everyone with a major's rank and above went home with a bearskin rug."

Polar bears, like all top predators, have a low reproductive capacity. Females breed every three years and give birth to an average of two cubs. Fewer than half of all cubs survive to celebrate a birthday. Recruitment into the polar bear ranks fell far short of the accelerated rate of hunting-based attrition.

By the early seventies, some estimates placed the total world population of polar bears as low as five to ten thousand animals. The alarm among scientists was so great, the outcry so loud, that it even forged scientific, then political, alliances that vaulted the Iron Curtain.

In 1973 a treaty was signed by five nations whose territories encompass the range of the polar bear—Canada, Denmark (Greenland), Norway, the USSR (Russia), and the United States (Alaska). The International Agreement on the Conservation of Polar Bears (known as the Oslo Agreement) banned the use of aircraft and icebreaking ships in the pursuit of bears and placed limits on commercial and sport hunting. The hunting of bears "by local people using traditional methods" was sanctioned by the treaty.

But isn't this amazing: that among the first cooperative steps toward a peaceful, post–Cold War era (and away from nuclear war) was a human concern for the survival not of our species but of another! One year after SALT I, two years after Ping-Pong diplomacy, there was Oslo.

The controls worked. Bear populations rebounded across the Arctic, including Churchill. By the 1980s, bear numbers were believed to have risen to between twenty and forty thousand. About this time, Churchill's bear-based tourist enterprise evolved. Initiated to meet the demands of professional and serious amateur photographers, it has flourished into a multi-million-dollar ecoindustry that sees thousands of eager tourists descend on this southernmost northern outpost every year.

Our group was one of these.

• • •

The bear continued to stare up at me with eyes as fathomless as they were benign. It was hard to believe that behind those eyes was the calculating mind of one of the planet's finest hunters and that behind his evident curiosity was a mind that was evaluating possibilities and calculating advantage.

As any good predator who hasn't eaten in four months would.

Me? Now that I was over my initial shock, and chagrin, I was captivated and thrilled. Since childhood I have been excited by, and sought out, wild things for no other reason than fascination. If getting up close and personal with a box turtle is fun, and watching deer from a tree stand exciting, try to imagine how exciting being within arm's reach of a polar bear is.

Not that such intimacy is limited to human imagination. That's what the worldwide ecotourist industry is all about.

We'd made our reservation for this polar bear expedition tour a year in advance. Demand is high. Competition for space in the Tundra Buggy Lodge, fierce.

Our group, numbering thirty-six participants, was divided into two subgroups: 78NS (naturalists) and 78NP (photographers). Linda and I were in the photography group because Linda is, after all, a photographer and because, since photographers tend to be very demanding, they usually get more than mere wildlife viewers. More time on station, better and less crowded conditions, closer proximity.

Even if we weren't photographers, we still would have paid the extra money and signed on with a photography group.

Our group ranged in age from thirties to eighties, with a median age of about sixty-five and participants from Australia, Japan, England, Canada, and the United States. Americans dominated. Most were retirees or people in the final stages of their professional careers.

At $5,500 per person, you can bet that most participants hailed from society's more affluent strata, as do those who are dedicated nature photographers.

With camera bodies costing between two and eight thousand dollars and lenses up to fifteen thousand, nature photography is not a poor man's game (but, based on my experience, a very good way to drive otherwise financially stable individuals into the economic lower ranks).

And equipment is just the down payment. Then comes travel, fueled by a desire to go to the beautiful and remote corners of the planet before it is all used up.

Rob Day, our genial, enthusiastic, and fiftyish leader, makes his living from photography. Rob is an Illinois native who specializes in backyard bird images. Bird magazines and bird feed companies rank among his main clients. Several other members in the group vetted their photos through "houses" specializing in nature photography, and one, at least, was working on a book.

"Oh, I hope I got some decent shots," Linda prayed, aloud, as our twin-engine prop started its descent into Churchill one cold, gray, snowy day in early November 2007—under the kinds of conditions photographers hate. Every photographer who is, or aspires to be, anyone ultimately comes to Churchill. Polar bears are almost rites of passage among nature photographers, must-haves in every photographer's portfolio.

If you ever purchased any of the calendars that are vended by the various conservation organizations, if you've ever seen one showing polar bears and willow thickets and spruce in the background, dollars to Klondike bars, you've seen a shot taken in Churchill.

Polar bears out on the open icecap? Without ear tags, radio collars, and vegetation? That's polar bears the hard way. And while Linda and I did see polar bears on Baffin Island, way back in June, the distance was too great for calendar- (or book-) worthy shots.

Polar bears in a town that lies at the same latitude as Juneau, Alaska, and has regular train service from Winnipeg, that's polar bears Churchill style. And while the polar bear express has made getting polar bear photos relatively easy, it still hasn't made it cheap.

We were two hundred feet over the runway before we even saw the ground. Late-morning temperatures were in the teens, winds were whipping the season's first snow into face-stinging fusillades. It might have been barely November, but winter was knocking on the door at Churchill.

In the plane, clad in avocationally sanctioned Arc'teryx, Mountain Hardwear, North Face, and Patagonia outerwear, we'd all nearly expired from the heat. Now on the ground, with many of us experiencing our first taste of winter temperatures, we were pleased to be loaded onto a waiting school bus. Hustled off to engage and be engaged by the many shops in Churchill that specialize in selling all things remotely related to polar bears.

Polar bear jewelry. Polar bear sweatshirts. Polar bear soapstone carvings.

"Tourism," I was told by the proprietor of a store that was about 70 percent polar bear chachkas and 30 percent budget-busting (but nevertheless beautiful) carvings, "is the jewel of Churchill. The more you polish it, the more it glows."

Most of the twelve to thirteen thousand–odd visitors that come to Churchill (more than ten times the town's population) are here expressly for the polar bear experience. The vast majority stay in hotels and lodges in town, where they board often crowded Tundra Buggies in the morning. Get on site around 9:00 A.M. Head back to town at 3:00. Some visitors may take only a single trip out to Polar Bear Point to see the bears before getting back on planes and retreating to warmer climates. With their near-requisite campaign sweatshirts and "I ♥ Churchill" key rings.

After our shopping opportunity in town, we were ferried to the Tundra Buggy depot, where at 4:30 we were allowed to board our vehicle. I counted fifteen buggies in all. Ours was driven by a genial young man named Chris, dressed head to toe in Mountain Hardwear.

A Tundra Buggy is a plywood-shod school bus sitting on tires built for earthmoving equipment with an industrial-grade gas-burning stove in the back. It's got school bus seats. (Need I say more?) It's got school bus windows—complete with raise up–lower down levers that you pinch until your thumbs turn white and that come screaming down when you hit a bump.

Which, of course, driving out on a road churned by several weeks of Tundra Buggy traffic, now frozen, you frequently do. Everybody, including and maybe particularly Linda, guarded their equipment on the twenty-five-mile, one-and-a-half-hour drive out to the Tundra Buggy Lodge. We were within sight of the lodge, whose lights were beckoning us in the near darkness of 5:30 P.M., when Chris sang out, "There's our first bear."

The animal was lying just off the road, with his nose between his paws and ample hams projecting into the air. A big white wedge of fur with button black eyes and Snoopy's nose.

We, of course, were ecstatic. The bear couldn't have cared less.

First Contact

My bear was beginning to show small signs of restlessness— or maybe resignation. My failure to extend my arm or get down from my perch in the name of interspecific harmony evidenced a disappointing degree of survival instinct.

"Have we met before?" I invited, hoping the sound of my voice would reboot the bear's interest. It did.

Craning his neck forward, nostrils flaring, the animal inhaled grandly, then exhaled a little puff of bear exhaust.

"Poooh," he as good as said.

"You're making that up, right?" I accused. "Well, I'm Christopher Robin. Pleased to meet you."

The bear didn't respond any more than to keep looking at me with those discerning and undisclosing eyes. The kind of eyes you see on age-darkened portraits. The kind of eyes that disarm you with detachment and neutrality.

The kind of eyes you can't lie to.

"Okay," I admitted. "Name's Pete. Pleased to meet you."

"Poooh," the bear said again.

What the heck. If I'd wanted conversation, I could have just stayed in the bar. But after six days, most of the stories worth telling and hearing had already been told and heard. The better and most recent ones were well known to me.

When we'd set out on our first morning of photography, nobody knew anything more about anybody than first names. After that extraordinary adventure, we knew everything down to how many frames per second their cameras were shooting and what expletives they favored.

Breakfast at 7:00, pancakes and eggs. Coffee, fair. Syrup, store-bought. Ketchup, in squeeze bottles, waiting on the table.

Outside temperature was about twenty degrees Fahrenheit. Skies, moribund gray. Bears, luke-active. A couple of small males roaming around in the glow of dining car lights, a mother with two disarmingly young cubs keeping her butt against the lodge and her eye on the male bears

By the time we clambered aboard the buggy, staking out strategic seats, Linda was as nervous as a frosh pledge at her first sorority mixer.

"Oh, I wish I'd brought Bertha," she moaned, cursing the "pack light" mentality instilled in her back in the days when carting stuff into the wilderness meant putting it on your back. Most ecotourists aren't burdened by this discipline, and most of the photographers onboard had one or more 500- to 600-millimeter lenses in their arsenals.

"The two-hundred-to-four-hundred is perfect," I assured her. "Much better for composing shots."

"Did you see the stuff some of the other people are using?" she pleaded, shaking her head in jealous disbelief. "There must be half a dozen Mark Twos and D Threes in this crowd."

For once, Nikon shooters outnumbered Canon users. The D3, Nikon's latest and greatest, is capable of shooting fifteen frames per second. Linda's D200, by comparison, is capable of only a measly, confidence-dampening five frames per second.

"Equipment's only as good as the person behind the viewfinder," I soothed. While this is true, based on the level of commitment it takes to get you and your stuff to Churchill (not to mention the very focused and practiced way everyone was setting up), it seemed that there were a lot of very accomplished photographers onboard.

At 8:05 Chris got us rolling. We rolled fifty yards (about the polar-bear-embracing range of a 600-millimeter lens) and stopped right next to the two males we'd seen at breakfast.

In about .00451 seconds every window went down (except the two that jammed). Sixteen cameras (soon to be joined by two more) were trained on the semi-indifferent bears, and while it was still too dark to shoot, everyone began shooting anyway.

It sounded like the crackle of electronic musketry.

clickclickclickclickclick; clickclickclickclickclick . . .

And this was only Linda.

Rob Day, marching up and down our ranks like a reincarnation of Wellington, was imparting wisdom and discipline to our ranks. Checking settings. Suggesting ISOs. Advising everyone to "take a couple of shots and then let me look at your histogram."

Linda was tense, firing in short bursts, biting her lips.

Linda never bites her lip, I thought.

clickclickclickclickclick; clickclick . . . clickclickclick . . . clickikikikik; clickkikikikik . . .

There were multiframe volleys to the left. Volleys to the right. And this was just the warm-up. Suddenly the two bears stood and began sparring. A photographer's dream. A *National Geographic* cover shot on the paw!

KAH-CLICKCLICKCLICKK'K'K'K'K'KKKKKKK . . .

"Watch your focus," Field Marshal Day warned. "Make sure you're getting eyes and heads."

"The bears weren't doing any of this last week," he confided to me after dressing the line. Satisfied that his troops had the situation well in hand. "It's the colder temperatures that make them more active."

After ten memory-card-filling minutes, the bears backed off, succumbing to bruin ennui, overheated in the twenty-degree air.

The photographers, nearly shell-shocked with elation, regrouped. Replaced memory cards. Changed lenses. Compared settings. Changed settings. Bemoaned the shitty light.

"Do you want to get in here?" Linda invited, nodding toward the vacant window, motioning toward her backup system waiting on the seat.

"No. And don't look now, but you're missing a shot," I counseled, nodding toward one of the bears, who was sitting up, sweeping his snout in the air, sniffing at a sudden, sanctifying burst of sunlight.

Linda spun. Said something expressively colorful. Started shooting.

The sound of her camera started a stampede for the windows, setting off a megapixel fusillade that would have rivaled a presidential press conference.

At 9:15 the first buggy in the stay-in-town tourist fleet arrived, pursued by nine more. The vehicles were crowded, two to a seat, the windows framed with eager faces hidden behind camcorders and pocket cameras.

"That other buggy is going to be right in our frame," one of our group growled.

"Buggy number nine," Chris called over on his radio, "you are going to be right behind our bears."

"Our bears!"

Damn tourists.

Suddenly the mother bear and her two cubs walked by, drawing all cameras. Then two new males showed up and began sparring. Virgin bears. Without ear tags! Everyone seemed paralyzed, torn between two once-in-a-photographer's lifetime shots.

I did a quick scan. There were now eleven bears around us. Seven shootably close.

And we were still only 150 yards from the lodge!

It was cold inside the buggy now. Exposed fingers clumsy with cold. Feet feeling the chilling effect of Arctic air that sinks to the floor while the heat of the stove rises to the ceiling.

"Anybody want to move and set up some shots?" Rob asked.

"YeahYeahYeahYeah . . ."

The panic was over. Everyone had shots to put on their Web sites and show the members of the photo clubs back home. Now it was time to concentrate on quality shots.

Bears on ice. Bears without willow branches in the background.

We traveled fifty yards before being forced to stop by photo ops just too good to ignore.

"There are so many damn bears here," someone said, expressing the problem.

A large male bear came up on Linda's window. Stood. She had to raise her lens hood to keep from hitting the animal's nose.

Her eyes were shiny and not from the cold.

The light and opportunities were so good now that even Chris, the driver, was driven to grab his camera and start filling cards. Rob had already surrendered to temptation.

At 11:45 we tried moving again. Not to find bears. But to

get a better angle on the sun (which had, unaccountably, begun to shine brightly). To accomplish this, we had to leave two sparring bears, two bears sleeping in the snow together, and the mother with cubs rushing at male bears.

Now we were parked south of the lodge, and Chris began ladling cups of butternut squash soup and handing out wraps. A tried and true strategy designed to guarantee a great shot. Sure enough, just when everyone had their sandwiches up and cameras down, mom and the cubs wandered over and started playing in the snow.

Tundra Buggies are big, their suspensions heavy duty. Still, in response to the human wave that rushed to the windows, our vehicle listed noticeably.

"I don't know how we're going to top this," a smiling Rob Day said to his sandwich (after filling close to a memory card of his own).

I don't know whether we ever did top the experience of that first day. But we matched it—every day that we went out. In fact, each successive day saw more snow, more and bigger bears, and better light. On the last day, so satiated were all onboard with their polar bear shots that we went off in search of willow ptarmigan.

Found them, too. Couple of flocks. White birds against white snow. Point-blank range.

There wasn't a photographer among us who wasn't happy to give the trip two thumbs up and sing the praises of the "Polar Bear Capital of North America."

And just like Rob said, we never even left the bus. Spent five days in an Arctic theme park. Enjoyed an intimacy with bears you could hardly match in an aquarium or a zoo, except that the animals were wild and free.

It was we who were caged. And while the intimacy was great, the disconnect was, too.

What we'd experienced was nature on our terms, not hers. It's not natural, but it is reflective of the growing disconnect between our species and the rest of the world. And I think, to a large degree, it explains why I'd elected to leave the group and find what I assumed would be solitude on the deck of the buggy.

What I found wasn't exactly communion. But at least it was disconnect from the disconnect.

THE WORLD ACCORDING TO POOH!

Animals don't commonly stand and stare into human faces unless they are intensely motivated. I've had deer pin me under their soul-piercing gazes for twenty minutes, wanting to know whether I constituted the threat they thought me to be. Our dog, Raven, can sustain an imploring look longer than any creature I've ever met, maybe indefinitely, but at least as long as it takes me to stop whatever it is I'm doing. Get up. Go to the closet. Get her the 4:00 P.M. dog biscuit.

But the bear, whose gaze was unwavering, was neither suspicious nor imploring nor any number of other attributes that we ascribe to, or divine from, other animals' expressions.

Not angry or fearful or nervous. Certainly not reproachful, or remorseful, or accusatory, or despairing, or vengeful, as a human might be, in the bear's situation, facing, as the species is, the ecological collapse of its world and possible extinction because of global warming. Projections are that the Arctic ice-cap will completely disappear in summer by 2050. Recent and more pessimistic estimates say sometime in the next decade.

One hundred years from now, a vestigial population of polar bears may still survive in the northernmost islands of the Canadian Arctic Archipelago, where they will live an ecologically partitioned existence similar to that of the polar bears of Churchill. Able to hunt the northern icecap that will still form in winter. Retreat landward when the ice melts in summer.

Those populations now living a totally marine existence will disappear. The bears whose range once bridged continents and time zones will be closeted in a corner of their former northern domain.

But the bear's eyes, like his mind, reflected none of this. He would, in his natural lifetime, certainly face the hardships imposed by global warming: the diminishment of resources, increased competition, possible starvation, maybe even drowning. But it was not the animal's problem to be burdened with this understanding. Understanding is a human affliction.

And maybe it was because the bear's gaze was so benign. Or maybe it was because, increasingly, I am seeing the world one way but still wanting it to be another. And it might have been just the wine.

But I suddenly found myself trying to explain things to the bear. Speaking to him, spirit to spirit, as the Inuit shamans do.

"It's like this," I said to the eyes. "It's not that we're a bad species, or a stupid species, or even an uncaring species. We're not."

The eyes didn't change expression. But my assertion didn't stop the bear from passing judgment.

"Poooh," he breathed.

"Okay," I admitted. "Maybe some of us are bad, and stupid,

and uncaring. But they're in the minority, and in America we believe in majority rule."

"We do care," I insisted. "Project the scope of our concern to include the earth and everything on it. Wrap whole not-for-profit organizations and government agencies around environmental protection. Limit ourselves with regulations and treaties to put a brake on human ambition. It's just that for a long time we didn't get the idea that we've been given this eco-tipping advantage, the capacity to manipulate whole environments.

"We're just beginning to understand that, when it comes to the earth's environment, we can dish it out faster than the rest of the planet can take it; that when we push something here, something unforeseen falls off an ice floe over there and . . ."

"Poooh," the bear observed, again.

Don't you just hate it when you are really trying to communicate and some adolescent bear calls your card like that?

"Okay, bear, I'll give it to you straight. The reason your world is collapsing and your species is toast is that, smart as we are, and caring as we are, when the chips are down, people don't care enough to be inconvenienced about something happening way up here, on the end of the earth, that doesn't have any obvious and immediate bearing on their lives.

"It's the same reason the rain forest is being leveled. Same reason 90 percent of the ocean's food fish have been depleted. Same reason aquifers are running on empty, the food column is riddled with toxins, and creatures as innocuous as frogs and as grand as tigers are being elbowed into extinction on my generation's watch.

"Sure, lots of people are sympathetic. But even people who spend a couple of weeks a year traveling to fabulous eco-destinations regard the natural world more as a playground than as the playing field that supports life on Earth.

"Most of the members of my species are too distracted and estranged to recognize, much less care about, the natural endowment that supports them, and the interconnectedness that binds them. Polar bears in the Arctic are far less pertinent than getting the car through inspection, making the monthly mortgage payment, or deciding what color to paint the kitchen—and, frankly, in this regard our species isn't much different from any other, big brain or no.

"We focus on what we have to do in order to advance and survive. Immediate needs trump long-term consequences, and let's not forget that the big brain evolved in order for individual protohumans to reach high-hanging fruit, not for all humans collectively to prevent deforestation or to keep the Arctic icecap from melting.

"So when we have mediocre leaders who tell us that the problem is exaggerated, the data inconclusive, we're willing to accept their assurance over our misgivings. It's what we want to hear. It's why we elected them in the first place and why candidates who espouse inconvenient truths come in second.

"When we get home after a hard day of reaching for high-hanging fruit and turn on the TV—and hear about sea levels rising faster than projected or famine spreading across sub-Saharan Africa—we solve the problem by changing the channel, switching to a network that assures us that climate change is part of a long-term natural cycle that's got nothing to do with us or the burning of fossil fuels.

"Now here's a word from our sponsor. The Fossil Fuel Coalition.

"And climate change is just too big a challenge to be solved by individuals alone. That's why we've got this system that brings collective wisdom to bear on problems that affect everyone. It is based on the premise that everyone is vested and that whatever a majority of the people want will be right. It works pretty well most of the time, but . . .

"But what happens when what the majority wants is to not be bothered?

"And if everyone is vested, doesn't that just make it easier for individuals to duck their personal responsibility and point the finger at everybody else?

"It begins with estrangement. It leads to denial and inaction. It's going to end with wholesale ecological changes and extinctions. So, bear, I guess what I'm telling you is that, unless you've got a fallback plan or can figure out how to de-evolve yourself into a brown bear in a couple of generations, it looks like an evolutionary dead end for bears that live on ice."

It was a long speech, probably the longest the young bear had ever heard. But the bear's equanimity was equal to his patience, and as a species that can wait next to a seal's breathing hole for hours, polar bears' patience is formidable.

The bear continued to regard me. But at least this time he didn't say "pooh."

I looked back at the sky. It was clear, still. The stars were shimmering brightly. Cassiopeia, the "seal oil lamp." The Big Dipper, "the caribou." The North Star, Nuuttuittuq, "never moves."

Never is a long time, but time and the heavens are never still. Because of the shifting movement of our solar system within the galaxy, in approximately twelve thousand years, Vega, the old woman coming to the rescue of the boy being chased by his knife-wielding uncle, is projected to replace the North Star as the polestar—the star directly in line with the axis of the earth. The new star that never moves.

Twelve thousand years. About as far ahead in time as the history of human habitation in the North American Arctic goes back. A long time to wait for a rescue.

Satisfied that my monologue was completed, the bear eased himself to the ground, a movement so quiet I had to look twice to be sure he wasn't still standing there. On noiseless feet he began moving into the night, a white phantom heading in the direction of the bay, which was, now, quickly freezing and would, until the end of June, constitute the center of the universe for polar bears.

"Hey, Pooh," I shouted, not at all sure why, except I didn't want to see the moment end; afraid, I guess, that this might be the last time I would see a polar bear in this life. Surprisingly, the bear turned, ambled back, and, as soundlessly as before, raised himself on his hind legs, pressed his paws against the steel side of the deck, bringing his face, again, close to mine.

"Good luck," I said. "I mean that. Stay away from the big guys until you gain a little more muscle mass, hear?"

I didn't say more, didn't try to put a better spin on the pronouncements I'd made. If polar bears are going to survive in this world of our making, then people, individually and collectively, are going to have to change. It is as simple and as difficult as that.

The bear, for his part, didn't linger. Once again, he dropped to all fours, turned, and headed in the direction of the bay, heading home. I watched until he was indistinguishable from the ice, until I heard footsteps and knew it was Linda coming to find me.

"Whatcha doin' out here, silly?"

"Thinking of some way to end the book. This will be the last chapter."

"Come up within anything?"

"Maybe. We'll see what it looks like when it goes down on paper. Dinner ready?"

We retreated to the dining room, two humans, a mated pair, who were, like the planet that supported them, moving from one season into another, moving toward winter.

Pooh? A strictly honest man would find it difficult to say. But being one of those animals equipped with the big brain and the power to conceive of possibilities beyond reason, I can tell you what I think and believe happened to the bear. The legend goes like this.

Pooh remembered the words of the tourist with the grapey breath. He bided his time, and, as the years passed, he grew large and strong, became a wily hunter and a fierce combatant. Females loved him. Seals surrendered their lives to him. No hunter ever got him in their sights. He vanished like a breath in the parched polar air.

"Poohf!"

He lived many years, outliving all of his kind, and when one day he discovered that the ice was almost gone, just as the tourist had predicted, he did not waste his strength searching needlessly but instead swam straight for the horizon.

Along the way he met the last ringed seal, who was searching for the ice and almost exhausted, and the bear said, "Come with me and live. There is no ice. The humans have been stupid. They used their intelligence to delude themselves. They stuck their opposable thumbs up their asses. We must survive until they are gone and the ice returns."

"Where are we going?" asked the seal.

"Into the sky," said the bear. "To live with the stars that bear our names."

So they swam to the edge of the sea and into the sky, the two animals whose lives are as close as life and death. The seal curled up in the lamp, near the center of the sky, where it could keep a watchful eye, and the bear joined Alcyone (who just happened to be female), where they amused themselves by sparring with the dogs and outwitting the hunters, waiting for the day when humans have outlived their stay, the ice returns, and they and all the creatures of the ice with it.

It is only a matter of time.

Bibliography

Akasofu, Syun-Ichi. "Secrets of the Aurora Borealis." *Alaska Geographic,* 29, no. 1 (January 2002).

"Arctic." Wikipedia, the Free Encyclopedia. http://en.wikipedia.org/wiki/Arctic.

"Arctic Ice Cap Could Completely Melt in a Decade." redOrbit, May 13, 2009, http://www.redorbit.com/news/science/1688397/arctic_ice_cap ...

"Big-Fish Stocks Fall 90 Percent Since 1950, Study Says." *National Geographic News,* May 5, 2003, http://news.nationalgeographic.com/news/2003/05/0505_030515_fishdecline.html.

Biological Response to Ecological Change Along the Arctic Coastal Plain. Alaska Science Center, US Geological Survey, June 2006.

Bourne, Joel K., Jr. "Fall of the Wild." National Geographic, May 2006, http://ngm.nationalgeographic.com/ngm10605/feature1/.

"Causes of Global Warming." EcoBridge. http://www.ecobridge.org/causes_of_global_warming.html

"Churchill, Manitoba." Wikipedia, the Free Encyclopedia. http://en.wikipedia.org/wikiChurchill_manitoba.

"Combustion." Wikipedia, the Free Encyclopedia. http://en.wikipedia.org/wiki/Combustion.

Contaminated Sites Program—Camp Lonely Landfill. Division of Spill Prevention and Response, State of Alaska, March 2005, http:www.dec.state.ak.us/SPAR/csp/sites/camp_lonely.htm.

De Tocqueville, Alexis. *Democracy in America and Two Essays on America*. New York: Penguin Books, 2003.

"Distant Early Warning Line." Wikipedia, the Free Encyclopedia. http://en.wikipedia.org/wiki/Distant_Early_Warning_Line.

"Dorset Culture." Wikipedia, the Free Encyclopedia. http://en.wikipedia.org/wiki/Dorset_culture.

Drew, Lisa W. "Unsafe Haven? Teshekpuk Lake." Living Bird, Winter 2008. http://www.livingbird.org/NetCommunity/Page.aspx?pid=267.

"Eskimo." Wikipedia, the Free Encyclopedia. http://en.wikipedia.org/wiki/Eskimo.

Feazel, Charles T. *White Bear: Encounters with the Master of the Arctic Ice*. New York: Henry Holt, 1990.

Fitzhugh, William W. "Vikings: The North Atlantic Saga." *AnthroNotes* (Smithsonian Institution), 22, no. 1 (Fall 2000). http://anthropology.si.edu/outreach/anthnote/Fall00/anthnote.html.

Hall, Edwin S., Jr. *A Review of the Cultural Resource Survey and Clearance Activities National Petroleum Reserve in Alaska 1977–82*. U.S. Geological Survey, March 1982.

Harden, Blaine. "Experts Predict Polar Bear Decline." *Washington Post*, July 7, 2005, http://www.washingtonpost.com/wp-dyn/content/article/2005/07/06/AR2005070601899.html.

"Inuit." Wikipedia, the Free Encyclopedia. http://en.wikipedia.org/wiki/Inuit.

"John River (Alaska)." Wikipedia, the Free Encyclopedia. http://en.wikipedia.org/wiki/John_River.

"Last Glacial Period." Wikipedia, the Free Encyclopedia. http://wikipedia.org/wiki/Last_glacial_period.

Lehman, Paul. Fall Bird Migration at Gambell, St. Lawrence Island, Alaska. *Western Birds* 36:2–55, 2005, Cape May, N.J.

"Little Ice Age." Wikipedia, the Free Encyclopedia. http://en.wikipedia.org/wiki/Little_ice_age.

"Lonely Long Range Radar Station." http://wilkimapia.org3717385Lonely-Long-Range-Radar-Station/.

MacDonald, John. *The Arctic Sky: Inuit Astronomy, Star Lore, and Legend*. Toronto: Royal Ontario Museum, 1998.

Mallory, Carolyn, and Susan Aiken. *Common Plants of Nunavut*. Nunavut: Nunavut Department of Education, Nunavut Wildlife Management Board, Canadian Museum of Nature, 2004.

McGhee, Robert. *The Last Imaginary Place.* Chicago: University of Chicago Press, 2007.

Miller, F. L., M. Rothfels, and D. Russell. *Caribou.* Hinterlands Who's Who. Ottawa: Canadian Wildlife Service, 1985, 1993, 2005.

Mull, Gill. "The Brooks Range." *Alaska Geographic* 23, no. 3 (1996).

"Nunavut." Wikipedia, the Free Encyclopedia. http://en.wikipedia.org/wiki/Nunavut.

Obbard, Martyn E., Trent L. McDonald, Eric J. Howe, Eric V. Regehr, and Evan S. Richardson. *Polar Bear Population Status in Southern Hudson Bay, Canada.* U.S. Geological Survey Administrative Report, 2007. http://www.usgs.gov/newsroom/special/polar_bears/docs/USGS_PolarBear_Obbard_SHudsonBay.pdf.

"Observed Climate Change." Arctic Climate Research at the University of Illinois, April 2008, http://arctic.atmos.uiuc.edu/.

"Petroleum." Wikipedia, the Free Encyclopedia. http://en.wikipedia.org/wiki/Petroleum.

"Photosynthesis." Wikipedia, the Free Encyclopedia. http://en.wikipedia.org/wiki/Photosynthesis.

"Pond Inlet, Nunavut." Wikipedia, the Free Encyclopedia. http://en.wikipedia.org/wiki/Pond_Inlet.

Pourchot, Patrick. Alaska Waterways: John River, September 12, 1974, http://www.outdoorsdirectory.com/boating/arl/john.htm.

Pielou, E. C. *A Naturalist's Guide to the Arctic.* Chicago: University of Chicago Press, 1994.

Pimlott, D. H. *Wolf.* Hinterland Who's Who. Ottawa: Canadian Wildlife Service, 1973.

"Polar Bear." Wikipedia, the Free Encyclopedia. http://en.wikipedia.org/wiki/Polar_bear.

"Polar Bear Status, Distribution & Population." World Wildlife Fund. July 2010. http://wwf.panda.org/what_we_do/where_we_work/arctic/area/species/polarbear/population.

"Polar Bear Status Report." Polar Bear International, 2010, http://www.polarbearsinternational.org/bear-facts/.

Reed, A., D. H. Ward, D. V. Derksen, and J. S. Sedinger. "Brant." *The Birds of North America,* no. 337 (1998).

Regehr, Eric V., Steven C. Amstrup, and Ian Stirling. *Polar Bear Population Status in the Southern Beaufort Sea.* U.S. Geological Survey Open-File Report 2006-1337. http://pubs.usgs.gov/of/2006/1337/.

Rey, H. A. *The Stars*. Boston: Houghton Mifflin, 1963.

Roosevelt, Margot. "World's Undiscovered Gas and Oil Is Largely North of Arctic Circle, Geologists Say." *Los Angeles Times,* May 29, 2009, http://articles.latimes.com/2009/may/29/nation/na-arctic-oil29.

Rozell, Ned. "Pondering the Process of Oil Formation Article #1335." Alaska Science Forum, May 1, 1997, http://www.gi.alaska.edu/ScienceForum/ASF13/1335.html.

"St. Lawrence Island." Wikipedia, the Free Encyclopedia. http://en.wikipedia.org/wiki/St_Lawrence_Island.

"Scientific Facts on Arctic Climate Change." Green Facts, 2004, http://www.greenfacts.org/en/arctic-climate-change/.

Steinbeck, John. *East of Eden*. New York: Penguin Books, 1992.

Stirling, I. *Polar Bear*. Hinterland Who's Who. Ottawa: Canadian Wildlife Service, 2003.

Struck, Doug. "NOAA Scientists Say Arctic Ice Is Melting Faster Than Expected." *Washington Post,* September 7, 2007, http://www.washingtonpost.com/wp-dyn/content/article/2007/09/06/AR2007090602499.html.

"Teshekpuk Wetlands Safe . . . For Now." *Issues Action*. Anchorage: Audubon Alaska. http://ak.audubon.org/issues-action/teshekpuklake.

Than, Ker. "The Mysterious Origin and Supply of Oil." LiveScience, October 2005, http://www.livescience.com/environment/051011_oil_origins.html.

"Tundra." Wikipedia, the Free Encyclopedia. http://en.wikipedia.org/wiki/Tundra.

The Tundra Biome. University of California Museum of Paleontology, 1994–2010, http://www.ucmp.berkeley.edu/exhibits/biomes/tundra.php.

Weller, Milton W., and Dirk V. Derksen. "The Geomorphology of Teshekpuk Lake in Relation to Coastline Configuration of Alaska's Coastal Plain." *Arctic* 32 (June 1979): 152–160. Pubs.aina.ucalgary.ca/arctic/Arctic32-2-152.pdf.

Wildlife and Oil Development at Teshekpuk Lake. Anchorage: Audubon Alaska, 2006.

"Yupik." Wikipedia, the Free Encyclopedia. http://en.wikipedia.org/wiki/Yupik.